How to Prepare A Business Plan

A Step by Step Guide

Peter Osalor

CONTENTS PAGE

PREFACE

My Life's Journey and Motivation

I was born into a family of six in the mid-1950's in Warri, Delta State, Nigeria. We lived in a mud house where there was no electricity and it was difficult to access drinkable water. My father was always in and out of menial jobs and at times, it was challenging for us to get a decent meal to eat. From an early age, I began to fend for my family by going to the water side to collect firewood to sell. Unlike us, neighbours and friends did not have to struggle to eat, some took their security to ready available food for granted and their parents would even discipline them or buy them multivitamins when they refused to eat.

I quickly realised that knowledge was key and began to dig deep, as I wanted to satisfy my growing curiosity on the big social differences in society. Why where some living in affluence and others in abject poverty? I had tasted poverty and hated it. It was this hate that fuelled my choice to live a life dedicated to finding out exactly why the world works the way it does.

I went to college as a house boy to a teacher because we could not afford to pay the school fees and that was the best the college could do for me. After college I went to work for Panalpina World Transportation Company in Kano. I bought a house for my mother and established a hotel for her. Then I bought a taxi, started a taxi firm and began to buy more vehicles, however I was not satisfied with my level of knowledge. I wanted more. I wanted to become a global entrepreneur, not merely a local one. I left for Britain in 1983, where I studied accountancy. While there, I took exams to become an accountant and began to apply the knowledge I acquired to various businesses.

By 1991 I was a chartered accountant and a chartered tax advisor. As I was investing in my global education in Britain, my wife and I bought two shops in 1995 but had to sell them by 1999 in order to fight bankruptcy.

In 2000, we established East London ITEC an IT and accountancy training institute. From 2001-3, I established branches of Peter Osalor and Co. in Port Harcourt, Warri, Yenagoa, and Lagos. We truly became a multinational global enterprise. Believing I could make a difference of the state of affairs in Nigeria, I ran for governor of Delta state in 2007 but was not elected. Throughout my entire journey, I have gained extensive experience in teaching, accounting, management, capacity and business building. Over time, I began to notice the consistent, predictable patterns and principles that appear to accompany and govern all business and career success. The most important of these principles is having an entrepreneurial attitude. This is what I aim to teach within the pages of this book. It is my desire to guide and mentor you to your path of becoming a successful entrepreneur.

My purpose in life has been the same for more than thirty years. It is to liberate the in-built potentials of individuals by giving them ideas and strategies to fast-track the benefits and rewards they can achieve as successful entrepreneurs. I intend to motivate people by making them realise that success is a choice they have to make and ANYBODY CAN BE SUCCESSFUL if they choose to be.

Putting into practice my vision for entrepreneurial development in Africa, I have established several initiatives:

- I have established **Success in Your Business,** *a UK registered charity committed to eradicating poverty by equipping individuals with the entrepreneurial spirit and the right skills succeed in business.*

- I have an on-line TV program

- As part of my awareness creation strategy for entrepreneurship, I run a weekly TV programme called Success in Your Business on African Independent Television, Abuja. A programme formerly aired on Ben TV London, NTA Warri and Port-Harcourt.

- I write a Business Blog. I am a regular columnist for the Vanguard Newspaper, commenting on the Nigerian economy and policy needs.

- I am a founding member of the African and Nigerian Entrepreneurs.com

- I am the CEO of Posag Consulting - a financial consultancy and business advisory service provider with offices in Nigeria, the United States of America and Europe.

- I have written several books on entrepreneurial success including: The Entrepreneurial Revolution: A Solution for Poverty Eradication, Why and How to Start your own Business, and How to write your Business Plan.

This book is written specifically for people who want to start their own business i.e. they want to become an entrepreneur; be their own boss and absolutely succeed. This book will teach you how to identify your passion and attract funds to manifest your passion as your business. More so, for people working in the business world who want to maximize their personal potential and get the best quantity and quality of business satisfaction, this little book will serve as a veritable compass. As you read, put into action what you read. Remember, if you do what successful people do, you will get the result successful people.

Best Wishes.

FOREWORD

One of the major socio economic issues confronting the Nigerian state is the high and rising number of the unemployed in the country. The problem is even more acute among the youth. Anecdotal evidence indicates clearly that the youth constitute the significant proportion of the unemployed and underemployed in the country.

The events of the last three decades have been characterized by some unprecedented uncertainty that has unusual threats as well as opportunities in the socio-economic, political, technological and competitive environments of businesses, which have automatically changed the frontier and landscape of the Nigerian entrepreneurs and enterprises. Retrenchments, retirements, restructure and re-engineering are now common features in the management of business enterprises.

This book is predicated on the philosophy of creating jobs by the entrepreneurs, emerging from the quagmire of unemployment caused by many years of mismanagement of the Nigerian economy. As entrepreneurs and potential entrepreneurs, this book will help you develop a well researched and easy to understand business plan. The book presents you a step-by-step guide to the different segments of a business plan without becoming overwhelmed with the process of developing a business plan.

The book is well written and clearly focused to tackle unemployment by meeting the challenges of doing business in Nigeria and the inculcation of the culture and spirit of entrepreneurship into the entrepreneurs, potential entrepreneurs and individuals. The book is made up of eight chapters which are well discussed. Peter Osalor's contribution will go a long way to filling the gap of lack of adequate texts in the area of how to prepare a business plan.

It is very easy to read and comprehend. It is therefore, a must for everyone practicing entrepreneurship, would-be entrepreneurs and the students who will also find the book indispensable as a reference material. It is our opinion, therefore, that the book will go a long way towards activating, cultivating and inculcating "entrepreneurship spirit" and culture into the readers.

Prof. Sarah O. Anyanwu
Department of Economics and
Former Director, Centre for Entrepreneurship
University of Abuja

FOREWORD

The economic turbulence in our world today which has made job securities to be volatile has probably created a ground swell for interest in business ownership and the expression of entrepreneurial skills. In spite of the presence of university education in our world for almost 1000 years, no school offered a degree in entrepreneurship until the 1970s. In the 70s there were only 16 universities that offered courses in entrepreneurship in the whole of the USA, today, over 1,600 do. Prior to that, every course directed people to learn how to manage a business on behalf of others. There are several reasons why the ownership of business is preferable to job seeking or the pursuit of employment.

A business gives you the opportunity to take your future in your own hands. Like they say in Latin Carpe Diem seize the moment. A business quite unlike employment can be inherited by your children, therefore giving you the opportunity to create generational blessings and prosperity for your family. That is why today we see the Ford Motor companies, Heinz, Rolls Royce, which was started by Mr. Rolls and Mr. Royce. The examples are endless.The best that can come out of employment is a salary and a possible pension. Whereas, a business can help you to build equity into the future. At a particular age, the statutory laws of employment of a country make your departure from gainful employment mandatory. While in your own business, you can continue to run in your golden age.

Furthermore, if anything makes the desire to have a business even more likable, it will be the fact that you can make a difference in your world as your company gets involved in corporate social responsibilities through the use of its profit or monies set apart to help meet social needs. You are able to provide employment for others and become part of the solution in your world. We might just rest our argument for business by saying that it helps you to leave a legacy.

However, what is the use having such a desire to run business and yet be poorly informed on how, why and which way to run it.
The author of this book, **Mr. Peter Osalor** takes us into the world of business by introducing to us four books that can set us in motion to start, perpetuate and run a successful business.

- Why and How to start your own business
- How to prepare a business plan
- How to identify and fund your business
- The entrepreneurial revolution – a solution for poverty eradication.

He brings in a fresh insight on the modalities for starting a business that will last. Yes, businesses that will last because 80% of businesses started here in the UK for example fail within 5 years. However, Peter has helped us with the effective steps that can help a successful business. He gives us a step by step guide on how to prepare a business plan and how to run it effectively.

Many businesses also die because they do not know how to leverage by seeking for funds that would make such vision run well. Using his training as a chartered Accountant and Tax specialist, Peter helps us to grasp the possibilities of a successful business as he gives us trade secrets for succeeding in the world of entrepreneurship.

The books of Peter Osalor come highly recommended firstly because of his educated mind. Secondly, because of the practical experience he has had with over 30 years of involvement in business and thirdly as a man who has opened up business in Europe and across Africa.
His experience traverses continents and any investment in this works will be more than value for money.

Matthew Ashimolowo
Speaker, Entrepreneur, Philanthropist

COMMENTS

In this book: How To Prepare A Business Plan – A Step by Step Guide" Peter Osalor, takes nothing for granted. The author carries through the rudiments of knowing what a good business plan is and how to prepare one. The book provides you a good understanding of why you must have a business plan thereby taming the roaming minds. You are made to know your markets, using good SWOT analysis. In the book, the author teaches you the step by step actions for anyone to write a good business plan and the common mistakes that need to be avoided. A worked example or model of a typical business plans was undertaken for the reader.

The book is indeed both a guide and a teacher. It is wholeheartedly received by teachers, students and professionals in economics, applied economics, finance and business management in every sector of life. It is a universal material which every one should read and keep in a good library.

Prof Park .O. Idisi
Departments of Agricultural Economics and Extension
Economics, University of Abuja.

ACKNOWLEDGEMENTS

To start with, I would like to thank God for enabling me make this book a reality, to Him alone be all the glory and honour. My profound thanks goes to my family, most especially my wife Mrs. Eudora Osalor who has always given me the support I have needed, every time I need it; your inestimable help is deeply appreciated. My daughter Peace Ani and her husband Chijoke Ani.

My thanks also go to Joseph Akpebu, a key member of my organisation for the relentless effort you have shown towards the production of this book, thank you so much. I would also like to thank Johnson Akpebu for his time and effort.

My sincere thanks also to Dr Abiodun Awomolo and Dr Hashim Gibrill both of Atlanta, USA, for their efforts in critically reviewing and helping put this book together. Mrs Ade D'Almeida for her contribution and inspiration and Pastor Matthew Ashimolowo my spiritual father and pastor, who has been a great source of inspiration in the writing of this book.

My sincere gratitude to Harry Koranteng, "my right hand man" for his time and effort.

To all my staff in London, Port-Harcourt, Warri, Yenagoa, Abuja and to Joseph and Hikmot Ademosu, I say many thanks for your support and commitment; you're all very much appreciated. Limitation of space does not permit me to individually acknowledge the innumerable number of friends and well wishers, thank you so much.

My message to you all is that this is just the beginning; the sky can never be our limit but only our starting point. Let's keep the fire burning.

Thank you

INTRODUCTION

"A winner translates dreams into reality, a loser translates reality into dreams."

Shiv Khera, Indian Motivational Speaker

Are you a winner? Do you have a dream to own a business? Are you seeking to translate this dream into reality? Like Shiv Khera states, only winners translate dreams into reality – whatever the cost. If you want to see your dreams become the reality of running your own business, you will need to put in work to make your dreams, reality. For many people, their dreams of starting their own business never leave the realm of dreams. They don't acquire the knowledge or skills required nor do they wish to put in the hard labour that it would take to make their dreams come true. They grumble and complain about how the government has let them down, how their relatives don't like them, or how nobody will lend them money to start their business. Fortunately, you think differently. You are a winner. You are prepared to do what it takes to translate your dreams into reality.

To run your own business, one of the basic things you will have to do, is write a business plan which gives you an opportunity to describe your products (goods and/or services), analyze your market strength, set up an operational and management team, create a workable balance sheet, and hopefully, attract investors. You use a business plan both to clarify your business to you and your team AND to communicate your business idea to outside entities such as investors, customers, and suppliers. This book will help you develop a plan for your business from the ground up. You will learn how to communicate your idea and passion in a clear and concise manner in order to win team players and funders.

You will gain insight into the many components of a business plan including market analysis, capital projection, budgeting, and operations and management. You will receive helpful tips and templates for writing your business plan in order to make your business easy to start. And if you already own your business, this book will offer you ideas to improve its quantity and quality. Remember, winners do what it takes to bring their dreams to reality.

The Entrepreneurial Development Series currently includes;

Volume 1 - Why and How to Start Your Own Business
A Simple Guide for Business Start-ups

Volume 2 - How to Identify and Fund Your Business
200 Business Ideas and 28 Ways to Raise Capital for Your Business

Volume 3 - How to Prepare A Business Plan
A Step by Step Guide

Volume 4 - Success in your Business
How to Become A Successful Entrepreneur

CHAPTER 1

"The only limits to the realization of tomorrow will be our doubts of today."

Franklin D. Roosevelt, 32nd President of the United States

THIS CHAPTER COVERS:

BEFORE YOU START

WHAT IS A BUSINESS PLAN

BEFORE YOU START

Before deciding to write a business plan, there are certain conclusions that you must have reached.

Here are few of them:

- You must have decided to go into business.
- You have your self assessment test if you are ready to be an entrepreneur.
- You have reasons why you want to go into business.
- You must have decided the type of business you want to do.
- You must have decided the medium.
- You must have known there is a need for your product/service.
- You must have decided how you want to fund your business.

The next step would be to incorporate all of these answers into your business plan.

WHAT IS A BUSINESS PLAN?

A business plan is a formal statement containing a set of business goals, alongside the reasons why they are believed to be attainable, and the plan for reaching those goals. It also contains background information relating to the organization, team or person attempting to reach those goals. A business plan can also be described as a document detailing an organisation's current status and plans for several years into the future. It generally projects future opportunities and act as a roadmap that shows the financial, operational and marketing strategies that will enable the organisation to achieve its goals. The focus of a business plan depends on the organisational concern. The content and format is influenced by the goals and audience in mind.

For a typical business (for profit), the business plan will typically focus on how products delivered will help reach set financial goals.

- Not-for-profit organisation might discuss the fit between the business plan and the organisation's mission.

- A Business plan for banks, need to build a convincing case for the organisation's ability to repay the loan and its associated interests.

- Venture capitalists are concerned about initial investment, feasibility, and exit valuation of the business.

Finally a business plan for equity financing will need to explain why the current resources, upcoming growth opportunities, and sustainable competitive advantage will lead to a high exit valuation.
A Business plan can best be described as the deciding factor between success and failure of a business, although a good business plan will not necessarily guarantee success, however it can go a long way towards reducing the odds of failure. A good business plan can help to make a business credible, understandable and attractive to someone who is not familiar with the business.

A typical misconception of most aspiring business entrepreneurs with regards to a business plan is that, a beautiful and a well presented business plan is the key to attracting funding and so look for secret formula for writing a winning business plan forgetting that a business plan is only worthwhile if it communicates a good business idea in a realistic way. Writing a business plan gives opportunity to an entrepreneur to discuss, debate and to decide on the direction of his/her business and to communicate this to outside parties.

If you want to speak the language of an investor then the key issues must be addressed, this book would enable you to craft a business plan that focuses on these issues.

CHAPTER 2

"Success is a state of mind. If you want success, start by thinking of yourself as a success."

Joyce Brothers, American Psychologist

THIS CHAPTER COVERS:

PURPOSE OF A BUSINESS PLAN

PURPOSE OF A BUSINESS PLAN

There is an old adage which runs: **if you fail to Plan, then you Plan to fail**. This adage applies directly to business. To become a successful business entrepreneur, before you embark on any business activities, you must make sure that you prepare a detailed business plan which depicts the blueprint for the business.

A business plan is vital for the following reasons:

- ***Fund-raising***

  With regards to raising funds for the business either from potential investors or some other sources, the business plan is usually the first port of call for anyone planning to make a financial commitment in to business. This will allow such persons to view the past present and future prospect of the business, one can safely assume it is the prototype of what the business is all about. Information contained therein will justify the reasons why they should or should not commit financially. Thus it should highlight core areas of interest such as financial projection, staff competency and business viability.

- ***Entrepreneur/Business owner***

  Preparation of a business plan is also significant for establishing strengths and weaknesses, therefore creating the ability to develop expertise and the financial risks involved in setting up a business.

- ***Keeping track/ managing performance***

  Business plan can be used to ascertain how a business is progressing. It represents continual process of planning and reviewing the performance of the business. It enables the owner in determining the progress of the business whilst checking it against the business goals, mission and or pin pointing any necessary improvement needed to keep abreast with current developments. Business owners see a business plan as a plan that should be updated, maintained, cross-checked, and used for the lifetime of a business.

- ***Supporting a company valuation at sale time***
  Although ascertaining value of a business is a difficult and a subjective process, the primary aim of the acquirer will be to access future income generation capability and the maximisation of their return, hence analysis of historic and future projections of the financial data in the business plan comes handy.

- ***Growth /Expansion/Diversification***
  A business plan describes an organisation's current status and plans for several years into the future. It projects the opportunities for growth, expansion and diversification including operational and marketing strategies that will enable the organisation to achieve it.

- ***Entering into a partnership***
  A partner to your business will be interested in the current and the future financial projections in your business plan.

- ***Business – other benefits of business plan***

- It gives you a sense direction and serves as action plan.
- Keeps you and your staff focused.
- Demonstrates the seriousness of your intentions
  to banks, investors, colleagues and employees.
- Sets targets and measures your success.
- Helps you recruit better and higher-level employees.

Before you begin to write your business plan, you must determine whether the proposed business plan addresses the following key issues (which basically constitute the initial assessment of the business):

People
Who are the people behind the business? What are their experiences? Are they known business entrepreneurs?

The opportunity
why did you choose that particular industry and how attractive are the opportunities in that industry. Who are the potential customers, suppliers, competitors? Are they any substitute products to your products and what are the barriers to entry into your industry?

The business model
What business model do you have in mind to exploit this opportunity identified? What are your sources of revenue and cash inflow? What are your costs drivers and the timing of outflow? What is the total investment required to make the business work? What are the critical factors for the business model and how long it will take to break even?

Strategy
How can you create a sustainable competitive advantage? What strategies are you going to adopt to market your product or services?

Context
What are the likely effect of changes in macro-economic factors on your business plan (interest rate, exchange rates, inflation etc.,)

Risks and rewards
What are the risks facing the business and what contingency plans have you got in place to mitigate those risks?

The answers to the above assessment should be portrayed in a plan that is written out in a logical order, easy to read, not too long and avoids complicated jargon.

The bottom line of failing to plan simply means planning to fail.

CHAPTER 3

"Every time you win, it diminishes the fear a bit.
You never really cancel the fear of losing;
you keep challenging it."

Arthur Ashe, Tennis Great

THIS CHAPTER COVERS:

MARKET ANALYSIS

SWOT ANALYSIS

MARKET ANALYSIS

One of the critical sections of the business plan is the market analysis. Every business plan should include market analysis; this is one of the first and most important reasons to do a business plan. Whether you are just starting a new business or reviewing an existing business, you should renew your market analysis at least every year updating to include market changes. A business needs to keep abreast with changes in the market.

Market analysis needs to look at the potential market, not the actual market served which is limited to your existing customers. The target market is much wider than just the people you already reach. They are the audience that are not presently being served which can subsequently be reached. These are the basis of the market analysis as it helps to identify the potential opportunities that a company could explore.

Getting information for your market analysis

Sources of information that will facilitate the production of a market analysis are different depending on the business plan. Information can be obtained from your local chamber of commerce, government statistics and commercial statistics or from internet searches. Not all information you need is going to be publicly available, and you may sometimes have to use information from educational publications, catalogues, industry, trade association and statistical compilations etc.

Segmentation

Always try to divide your target market into useful segments. Dividing the market into these segments will help the company to address specific market needs, media, pricing patterns and decision criteria in each of their different market segments. Segmentation helps you target specific people with specific messages and helps you focus on user needs. Knowing your market segments will help you make smart decisions when it comes to providing the products and services that will work best for them and for communicating with them.

Market size and growth

It is necessary that size and growth of the market can be weighed and quantified. Knowing the number of people in your market, be it hundreds or millions and the ability to show what the total market is, for your business must be considered.

When it comes to market growth, the focus is about percentage change as a market forecast. You need to able to determine whether the number in your target market is increasing or decreasing and be able to quantify this annually?

Market forecasts start with the total numbers of possible purchasers in each market segment, then projected percentage change over the next three to five years.

Market trends

You need to understand what is going on with your market. What trends and fashions do you see having an influence on your market segments? The questions that affect target markets will be different for every business. A crucial aspect as you create your business plan is that you become aware of the market trends that affect your specific market.

How to research the market

Before you get the research ball rolling, you need to come up with a solid business concept. Once you have a concept, you need to determine if it is viable. You need to do some research before taking the plunge. First find out if there is a demand for your product or service. Do a competitive analysis and create a plan which differentiates your product or service from that of your competitors.

Information is fundamental in developing a unique business proposition that will give a company an edge over competition.

The best sources of information will vary depending on the type of business and the circumstances, but options include the following:

Trade information
Trade associations or unions, online trade publication, union manuals, trade shows.

Demographic and economic data
Government portals which enables you to find out information on things like age range, income, number of businesses by type in a geographic area and the total sales in your category.

Business groups
Local chamber of commerce and government sponsored small business development centres which assist entrepreneurs.

Local universities
Graduate students do market feasibility study for course credit.

Local competitors
Find a similar business in a similar city and ask to talk to the owner and also look at similar business for sale and contact the brokers for information like why they are selling and what their financials are like.

National competitors
Do online search of business in your industry and evaluate what they offer-tune your idea

Potential customers
Run your idea up the flagpole with informal focus groups. Talk with friends and old customers.

To figure out if you should go ahead with your business idea, you need to ask questions like these:

- Is the market saturated? – is there room in the market for one more business?

- Is there a demand for your particular product/ service?

- What are the competition doing? -What do they do well? What do they do poorly? What is unique about them?
- Can you offer something different that will encourage customers to patronise you instead of more established businesses.

- Can you reach your target audience?

COMPETITOR ANALYSIS

The key to winning market share is to differentiate your company by providing products, services or solutions that your best prospects will find more desirable than what's offered by your closest competitors. Experienced marketers know it is always easier to fill a need than to create one. Someone who is already using the type of product or service you offer is a great prospect because he or she has a clearly defined need and can afford the purchase.
The job of convincing qualified prospects to buy from you instead of your competitors is where real work begins. These simple four step competitive analysis will help you in analyzing your competitors.

1. Do some detective work
Observe their web pages, print and broadcast advertising, and articles in which your competitors have been featured. Depending on your industry, you may also be able to do some mystery shopping, which will allow you to experience what it's like to shop and buy from companies that sell similar products or services.

2. Evaluate "perceived " competitors

Chances are, you have a lot more competitors than you think. In addition to real competitors evaluate the marketing tools and materials of any businesses you perceive as offering a similar set of products or services.

3. Focus on the message

Once you have gathered the materials, the next step is to analyze what is being communicated and how. Identify the key promises made by your competitors. You may find the majority of your competitors have similar messaging, with only a few front runners showing strong points of differentiation. After assessing the most effective messaging, look at the actual tools and materials, what formats seem to work best overall? At this point, your competitive analysis will reveal whether your company is lacking any standard tools that prospects expect everyone in your industry to offer.

4. Find a unique spin

It all boils down to this: how will your company satisfy its customer's needs in a way that is both unique and compelling? Consider not only the products or services you sell, but also how the company operates, including particular features i.e. characteristics, standard of customer service etc.

Assuming there are no particular features that gives your product/ service an edge above the competition, then the use of information gathered from the competitive analysis can be employed to create uniqueness about what the company sells and how it is sold.

SWOT ANALYSIS

SWOT analysis evaluates your strengths, weaknesses, opportunities, and threats. A SWOT analysis should have a place in every entrepreneur's strategic toolbox. Whilst it is not something you will do daily, having the analysis can give you a basis for guiding all sorts of actions on a continuous basis.

With every decision you make, filter what you are good at and what you are not so good at. Consequently this will subconsciously apply SWOT to your decision-making process.

SWOT analysis essentially consists of brainstorming about the key variables that affect your company.

- Strengths may include special skills, motivation, technology, or the distribution or financial capacities that you possess.

- Weaknesses are negative factors, such as lack of capital, shortages of skilled personnel or unproven products.

- Opportunities are positive circumstances that, if exploited, will boost your company's success. They may include untapped markets, promising customer relationships and weak competitors.

- Threat factors should include not only clearly visible threats, such as pending regulations, but potential problems, such as economic downturns, new competitors or changes in consumer tastes.

There are two main goals in a SWOT analysis. First you want to identify areas where your strengths match your opportunities. For example, a low-cost producers' strength can be matched with an opportunity in the existence of an untapped cost-sensitive market.

Secondly, recognize areas where weakness makes you vulnerable to threats. For instance, if there is a trend toward more regulation in your industry and your business has an image as an outlaw that could be a problem. Results of the analysis can be used to establish specific moves that will enhance strengths, maximize opportunities, remedy weaknesses and defuse threats.

CHAPTER 4

*"To guarantee success, act as if it were
impossible to fail."*

Dorothea Brande, Writer

THIS CHAPTER COVERS:

STEP BY STEP GUIDE OF HOW TO WRITE A BUSINESS PLAN

STEP BY STEP GUIDE OF HOW TO WRITE
A BUSINESS PLAN

There are some basic elements that must be covered in your business plan to make it attractive to whatever purpose you intend to use it for. It is necessary that all sections must interrelate and not isolated in any way.

A good business plan should be designed to answer the following questions:

- Why does your business exist? (purpose or mission statement)

- Where do you want to take it? (objectives)

- How will it get there?(strategy)

- What will it cost?(budget)

Although there is standard structure for a business plan, no two plans have identical headings, flows, and appendices. Some of the contents will have different names and presented in different order. Every successful business plan should include something about each of the following areas, since these are factors which make up the essentials of a good business plan:

1. Executive summary

The most important section of the business plan is the executive summary. It gives the reader an idea of what to expect in the rest of the plan. Most business plan readers, after reading the executive summary will decide whether to proceed further or discard the plan.
Be brief by making sure that every word has earned its place. Highlight the benefits that the business will add to the reader,

demonstrate that the business will be able to meet its long term financial obligations and also emphasis the benefits and privilege associated with **hanging** out with you, and the possible loss of not.

You must endeavour not to exceed two pages and should comprehensively and eloquently summarise the most important aspect of the plan to the bare minimum. It is advisable the executive summary should provide readers with a quick overview of the whole report. The summary should adequately cover:

- The company (who, what, where, when)
- The management and their strengths
- The business objectives and why it will be successful
- If the business needs financing, why you need it, how much you need and how you intend to repay the loan or benefit the investor

2. General company description

The general description section covers the overview of the principal activity of the business. There is no need to be detailed in this section as there are other sections which will allow you to give details on the overview. Normally one to two pages should be adequate for this section. The introductory section should cover:

- Name of the company, type of legal entity, ownership, significant assets
- Mission statement of the business
- Company goals and objectives
- The main features of the industry in which you will operate
- The most important company strengths and core competencies

3. The opportunity, industry and market

This section expects you to exhibits your knowledge or insight of the industry, the market and the opportunity from the research you conducted before writing the business plan.

a) The opportunity

In this section you give facts as to what inspired the business concept, explain precisely the exact issue that currently needs to be addressed i.e. is there a new problem that you are trying to solve, existing problem or new benefits. This section should include:

- Where is the gap in the market?
- What has given rise to this gap?
- How was this gap identified?
- How will the gap be filled?

b) Industry

This section describes the major players and their influence on the smooth operation of the business. Usually it discusses the barriers to entry, suppliers, customers, substitute products and competition. Answering the following questions will be appreciated.

What are the barriers to entry in this industry?

You need to consider high costs, high production costs, high marketing costs, consumer acceptance and brand recognition, extensive training and skills, unique technology and patents, tariff barriers and quotas, legislation or regulation.

- How will these barriers be overcome?
- How much power do the customers have?
- Who are the customers?

- Do they have significant power or influence over the prices they pay?
- Do they have significant choice when buying the product or service?

How much power do the suppliers have?

- Who are the suppliers?
- Do they have significant power or influence over the prices they charge?

Are there a limited number of suppliers?

- Are there substitutes for the product or service?
- What is the likelihood that consumers will switch to a substitute product or service? Are there any indirect competitors?

Who are the competitors and how strong is the competitive rivalry?

- What products and companies will compete with you?
- How will your products or services compare with the competition?

What are the major changes affecting the industry?

- Consider changes in technology and government regulations

c) Market

This part of the plan should contain detailed information about your target market which your products or services are intended for by addressing the following questions:
- What is the size of the market?

- How fast is the market growing?
- What percentage share of the market will you have?
- What are the major trends in the target market – trends in consumer preferences, demographic shifts and product development?

4. Strategy

Whilst your strategy may be flexible, it should be grounded in thorough market research. Various business analysis technique can be used on strategic planning including SWOT analysis (Strengths, Weakness, Opportunities, and Threats) or PEST analysis (Political, Economic, Social and technological analysis), etc.
This section should illustrate the scheme proposed to compete and outwit your competitors in your chosen market. Below are some of the issues that will serve as a guiding principle.

- The focus of the business: broad mass market or a specific niche?
- How the business will succeed in the market?
- How will you create a unique and valuable position, involving a different set of activities?
- What is the value for the customers? Describe the value proposition for the customer?

5. Business model

It is central to a business success. It indicates how the business will be generating profit or revenue. Business model should comprise a consolidated framework including sources of revenue.

- How does the business generate income or revenue
- The major costs involved in generating the revenue
- The profitability of the business(revenue less costs)
- The investment required to get the business up and running

- The success factors and assumptions for making the profit model work
- List the factors that are critical success factors of your business

Building a business model

These questions force you to focus on how the business will generate revenue. When thinking about these question it is important to:

- **Identify the target customer** who will buy your products or services? Be specific in identifying your target customers by their demographic profile, where they live, their preferences and what will trigger their decision to buy.

- **Be specific about the value you will be providing to the customer** what benefit will they get from the goods or services you are selling to them? The clearer you are about the exact value that customers can expect, the easier it will be for you to sell the goods or services. The value that you provide should be communicated in all marketing materials that goes out from the company.

- **Be clear on the number of revenue streams you will have in your business** some business have more than one revenue stream and there is a different set of customers attached to each revenue stream. You must make sure you are able to identify them clearly.

- **Be specific about the price** what do you expect to charge for your product or service? Knowing this will enable you to evaluate whether customers perceive that they are getting value for money and also to determine if profit can be made from selling at your intended price.

- **Recognise the timing of expected income from sales** will you collect revenue before or after sale? Will the revenue be collected at once or over a period of time?

How to fine tune your business model to increase revenue

To make your business model more innovative from an income generating perspective, you need to consider these questions:

- Are there people or businesses that could use my goods or services but don't currently have access to them? Would it be beneficial for me to reach out to such a group?

- Are there people who are not buying what 1 offer due to price? If 1 shifted the price point up or down and adjusted my offering could 1 tap into a whole new market?

- Is everything you are doing for customers providing them with value? In what areas can cost be reduced without customers' perception of value?

- Are there additional untapped revenue streams that you could exploit?

- Are there ways that you could alter the timing of revenue collection to benefit the business? Smaller business benefit by getting cash in earlier to speed up cash flow.

Thinking about your business model can be an excellent source of clarity, focus, innovation and differentiation. Too few entrepreneurs take time to clarify issues such as their target market, what they are going to do to make the money, what their major cost drivers are what they can do to minimise those costs?

Entrepreneurs, who do not engage in a detailed research to address these issues, are more than likely to operate their business hazily due to lack of tangible information. Such people go into business based simply on exploiting an opportunity without fully analysing whether it will make a profit. The discipline of defining and articulating your business model will help you streamline your business so that you only engage in activities that positively contribute to the bottom line and assist you in identifying activities that seek to use resources, are inefficient and unproductive overall.

6. Team-Management and Organisation

1.

These portray the skill, experience and qualification of people behind the business. It should include:

- A list of the founders including their qualifications and experience
- A description of who will manage the business on a day-to-day basis
- What experience do these individuals bring to the business?
- What special or distinctive competencies do they offer?
- An organisational chart if you have more than 10 employees showing management hierarchy and responsibility for the key functions

7. Marketing Plan

This will illustrate all the components of the marketing strategy inclusive of product positioning.

It needs to disclose the important marketing decisions about:

- The product or service and why it is valuable to customers
- The focused and detailed description of the target market
- The positioning of the product or service- how it should be

perceived by customers

- The pricing strategy with specific price points at which the product will be sold
- The sales and distribution channels that will be used to get the products or service to the customer
- The promotion strategy including public relations activities, specific promotions, advertising and intended viral marketing activities

8. Operational Plan

2.

This section explains the daily operation of the business, its location, equipment, people, processes and surrounding environment.

This section should discuss:

- A description of the operating cycle that describes what the organisation will do to deliver its service create and sell its product
- A description of where all the necessary skills and materials will be sourced
- What will be outsourced, what relationships are in place and how those relationships will be managed
- The cash receipts and cash payment cycle of the business

9. Financial Plan

3.

A Financial plan is a reasonable estimate of company's financial future. Make sure you don't include too much detail in the main body, but rather, include detailed projections and supporting calculation as an appendix. Apart from these, you'll also need to know the critical ratios in your industry when writing business plan. You can get them by looking at the available financial statements of companies in your industry. If you do not have the basic accounting knowledge, get an accountant.

The following are the most important document that should be
included in the financial plan:

- Start-up expenses and capitalisation – which describes and
  explain what it will cost to launch the business and where
  you expect to get this money
- 12- month profit and loss projection – month-by-month and
  a three-year profit and loss projection (quarter-by-quarter)
- A 12-month cash-flow projections and a three-year cash-
  flow projection (quarter-by-quarter)
- A projected balance sheet at start-up and at the end of years
  one to three
- A break-even calculation

10. Appendices

4.

The Appendix section should include additional supporting
documents that the reader may refer to.

Documents expected to be the appendix are:

- Brochures and advertising materials
- Industry studies
- Blueprints and plans
- Maps and photos of location
- Magazine or other articles
- Detailed lists of equipment owned or to be purchased
- Copies of leases and contacts
- Letters of support from future customers
- Any other materials needed to support the assumptions in
  this plan
- Market research studies
- List of assets available as collateral for a loan
- Detailed financial calculations and projections

CHAPTER 5

"Don't ask what the world needs. Ask what makes you come alive and go do it. Because the world needs people who have come alive."

Howard Thurman, Author, Philosopher

THIS CHAPTER COVERS:

ATTRIBUTES OF A GOOD BUSINESS PLAN

ATTRIBUTES OF A GOOD BUSINESS PLAN

A good business plan tells an interesting and comprehensive story that an outsider can use to evaluate the viability of a new or an existing business concept. This chapter looks at what should be put in a business plan that will inspire confidence in investors or for whatever purpose it is meant for.

The following outline what should be in a business plan:

- **Make a strong first impression**

A business plan is a reflection of people behind the business. Formatting, spelling and visual appeal contribute to the impression that investors form about the business entrepreneur. Business plan with contents that has spelling and formatting errors, gives an impression of a business entrepreneur who cannot take the time to put together a worthy business plan then how can that business entrepreneur take time to get grips with the million other less important details it takes to build a business case.

Keep the business plan simple, use white A4 paper , a simple 12 point font like Arial and numbered pages. I have seen an excellent business plan with only 6 pages in length and a terrible one with over 50 pages long. It is necessary to include information in your business plan on a 'a need to know' basis".

- **Succinct overview**

Many investors rely heavily on an executive summary to make an initial evaluation of the business plan hence it is of utmost importance to provide a short ,precise and to the point business overview giving the investors a profile of the business as well as a description of the product and services being offered.
Write a good one-page executive summary. There is a good chance

that the potential investor or your target would not even read any further if this is not compelling.

- **Coherent and complete**

Business plan must link together in a coherent way and all the relevant issues need to be addressed. The content of each section of the plan must correlate effectively to the information in the other sections. Researching enables you think through all the issues necessary for the business to be successful. To make a business plan coherent and complete the business entrepreneur must write the business plan himself or must be involved from the beginning to the end as no one knows your business better than you. The service of a consultant may be employed however the whole process should not be outsourced.

- **Focus on financials**

Investors are especially interested in the financial prospects of a business. Investors pay a great deal of attention to the financial forecasts in the business plan. The financial plan should be realistic and understandable; the assumptions underlying the projections should be clearly outlined and justified. It must be noted that of all the financial projections, cash flow is the most critical.
The high incidence of business failure within the first year, points amongst other things to a serious of lack of financial knowledge amongst business entrepreneurs. You can outsource your financials if you are not a number guru, but that does not mean you can abdicate from the responsibility to understand what they mean and make sure they are accurate and reflect real possible business path.

In reality you should understand the finances inside out –those that do, may well hold the key to success and prosperity.

- **Business model**

Different factors account for success across different kind of businesses. It is imperative to assess other business models in your industry. Devise and fine-tune a practical model that will work for you. In the business plan the entrepreneur must demonstrate that they understand what is unique about their business, individualise it with their own brand that will differentiate it from others whilst keeping in mind that it needs to be workable and not merely an impressive theory and that they have the model in place to achieve it.

To demonstrate the deep understanding of the proposed business concept, you must be able to describe a typical customer, the product and exactly how it is going to be marketed.

- **Promote people**

The business plan must reflect a winning team. Be specific about who is involved in the business, what role they will play and what skills and experience they possess to make them effective in their role.

- **Match with mandate**

Entrepreneurs must do a 'due diligence' on their target or investors. Go to their website and study about their investment criteria, understand their investment process, look at their investment portfolio, read some press releases and articles, ask around if anyone you know who has dealt with them before. If possible, contact the potential investor before just sending off a business plan. If you know what investors are looking for before you start writing a business plan, you will be in much stronger position to produce a document that inspires confidence and even excitement.

- **Operational plan**

Ascertain or identify the five top operational success factors for the business and explain how you are going to handle each one on a practical level. Don't forget things don't happen by themselves.
For operational plan to be successful everyone in the business must know exactly what is expected of them. One way of achieving or ensuring its success is to have a briefing and a debriefing session at the start and close of work.

- **Marketing plan**

The essence of marketing is about getting the message to your prospects not the entire population of the country. Advertising costs lots of money, think smart and adopt a cost effective medium of advertising like leaflets, SMS marketing , direct selling and as much as possible avoid ideas of big advertising campaigns , billboards and radio unless you have the money. Marketing represents a client or customer's holistic view of your business, it is therefore of paramount importance not to ignore your marketing process.

- **Layout and presentation of the plan**

Always keep it simple. White A4 paper, a simple 12 point fort like Arial, numbered pages as short as possible. You can ask a knowledgeable person to edit the copy as it is unprofessional for a business plan to be full of spelling mistakes. You can also consider an accountant to help you compile realistic financial forecasts.

- **Pitching and presentation the idea**

The biggest mistakes people make is to oversell. They want to tell the whole story in the first meeting. It is advisable to tell just enough of the story that shows you know what you are talking about and are going to make it work, with or without the investor. Make sure when you have pitched enough to intrigue the listener, stop talking and let them think and ask questions remembering that you want to be at an intersection, not going down a one way-street.

CHAPTER 6

*"It's not what you have; it's what you do with
what you have."*

Anonymous

THIS CHAPTER COVERS:

BUSINESS PLAN MISTAKES TO AVOID

BUSINESS PLAN MISTAKES TO AVOID

Writing a business plan is not without its problems. The essence of this chapter is to identify and find ways to get around them.
The potential problems encountered are as follows:

- **Business plan not specific**

Be specific and not be vague, don't forget investors want to know exactly what their money is going to be use for. Also remember, investors have several investment options, of which yours is one. It's always essential to bear in mind that, writing a business plan is a blueprint for your business's work over the next one to three years. You have to be specific as to the main purpose of the plan. If it is to seek investment in the business it is important to clearly describe the investment opportunity. There is a tendency for entrepreneur to focus myopically on the product; it must also address the purpose of the plan. Once the primary objective of the plan is clear and specific, the entrepreneur will be able to ensure that the key requirements of the reader are met.

- **Lack of information about the market**

Most new business entrepreneur often neglect to research about the market, the competition or even who might actually pay for their products. They dive headlong into writing up a business plan and don't want to spend money on research by third parties. At least you can do the most basic research on the internet and directories to give you an idea of the market.

Opportunities are only prospective ones without the evidence that the target market can be accessed profitably. It is important that, the business plan includes a detail comprehensive and credible analysis of how the business intends to secure access to their target market in a cost effective manner. Knowledge of who the customers are, and how they buy is important.

- **Inaccurate Finance Forecasts**

Don't delude yourself with wild figures that in all probability will never happen. There is no need of being optimistic to convince investors to give you some money. If your business fails to live up to expectation as projected by the financial forecast, it will make it difficult, as money expected is not forth coming. When forecasting financial project, bear it in mind that reality turns out better than forecast.

The fact that figures are projected does not mean they can be included without rigourous process. They need to be credible, defensive and consistent. It is paramount; that these figures confirm the company ability to generate free cash flow so that the business can be run profitably while satisfactorily servicing their debts at the same time.

- **You don't know who to ask**

Sometime it is difficult to get an advice for the input into your business plan. In terms of small companies you can ask everybody. For big companies it is impractical but you can still invite ideas by form, internet, written down. Give people the opportunity to see the current business plan and ask them what they think, their contribution and encourage participation to make them feel part of the whole business.

- **The plan contains mistakes**

It might make a difference between an investment and none. If the business plan is sloppy and contains mistakes, it gives a bad image and the kind of business you might operate. The best idea is to get two or three pairs of eyes to go through and vet the plan.

- **Lack of a viable opportunity**

A business plan needs not only describe opportunity, but it must also detail how the opportunity can be exploited profitably and demonstrate the business ability to deliver what is required.
Once they are detailed, there will be greater transparency regarding viability, opportunity in terms of company's ability to profitably serve the target market.

- **Overestimation of revenues**

Entrepreneurs have the tendency to exaggerate every business opportunity. At a point in time, those figures will need to be justified and if it emerges that they are mere fantasy, the potential investors will lose all credibility and it will significantly undermine any confidence they might have in your plan.
Placing some rigour around the process of deriving credible revenue figures also serves the entrepreneur by enhancing their awareness of some of the key drivers for revenue growth in their business. Apart from that, it will also help to produce a more plausible business plan, which enables the entrepreneur to answer any questions credibly with regard to the market opportunities.

- **Lack of appreciation for the importance of a good cash flow management**

Insolvency is the most significant threat to business. It is therefore critical for entrepreneurs to understand the differences between cash and profits. Most business fails, not because they are unprofitable, but rather as a result of their insolvency, (inability to pay debts as they fall due). Good cash flow management is vital when business pursue investment opportunities. A well structured business plan needs to reflect the reality with likely losses in the first months expected and with financing provisions.

A contingency figure should also be added as it is important to leave breathing space for the unexpected costs and overspends that always occur when least expected.

This is about planning, not accounting, and you are only guessing the future in an environment full of uncertainties.
As important as monthly details are in the beginning, they simply become unnecessary later on. How can one project for monthly cash in the next three years from now, based on uncertain sales forecast?
A plan can be made for 5, 10 or even 20 years into the future based on theory however it is unrealistic to plan in monthly detail past the first year. This is not expected and neither is it rational.

- **Don't create absurdly optimistic "hockey stick projections" of sales taking off in near future**

Optimism is wonderful nevertheless it ought to be justifiable in essence it needs to contain an element of pragmatism in other words assuming that once funding is available sales will automatically sky rocket is setting up for a huge disappointment. This is not to say it is impossible, it probably happens once a generation. Investors desire and deserve to have factual projections that are credible.

- Don't exceed 25 pages. Don't write too much
- Detailed financial projections should not be excessive
- Minimal use of technical jargon

CHAPTER 7

"All great achievements require time."

Maya Angelou, Poet

THIS CHAPTER COVERS:

MODEL BUSINESS PLAN

MODEL BUSINESS PLAN

BUSINESS PLAN FOR ELECTRONICS SHOP, TESCO ELECTRONICS LTD

Executive Summary

Tesco Electronics is a start-up business located in the Central end of Jamestown. The company specializes in the repair and sales of home electronics, specifically home entertainment electronics, including TV, DVDs VCRs and CD players. We will target people who place great importance in their entertainment equipment and own higher-end electronics, where repairing them would be more cost effective than replacing them. Many low end VCRs for example, are priced so low, people find it more cost effective and convenient to purchase a new product than to get the existing one repaired.

The company is owned and managed by Sammy Jay, with a degree in electrical engineering from the University of technology. He is a certified electronics technician with various brand companies. He will also employ his son to help with running and growing the business.

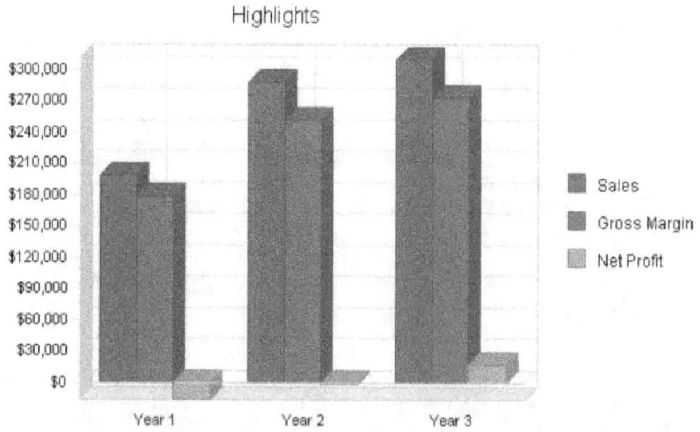

1.1 Objectives

Tesco Electronics (TE) is a growth-oriented business. Its ten year goal is to become a regional leader in TV/VCR/home stereo repair, with shops in the Jamestown. With this in mind, the objectives over the next three years for Tesco Electronics are the following:

- Achieve steady growth in sales revenues by year three.
- Achieve local market share (in the Jamestown area) of approximately 20% by year five.
- Expand product line to include authorized satellite service installation and new home entertainment electronics sales.

1.2 Mission

The mission of Tesco Electronics is to provide high quality, convenient and comprehensive TV/DVD/VCR and home electronics repair at a low cost. The most important aspect of our business is trust. It is the goal of our firm to have 100% customer satisfaction in regards to quality, friendliness and completion time, and discover new ways to exceed the expectations of our customers while doing so at the lowest possible cost.

1.3 Keys to Success

In the TV/VCR repair industry a company builds its client base on one customer at a time and mostly through established marketing practices (ads, billboards, etc.). With this in mind, the keys to success for Tesco Electronics are:

- High-quality work.
- Attention to professional appearances at all times.
- Knowledgeable technicians that are friendly, customer oriented, and will take the time to explain to customers the intricate nature of our business and our work.

- Maintaining a highly aggressive managerial oversight on costs to provide our services at the lowest price.

Company Summary

Tesco Electronics is envisioned to be the low cost leader in TV/DVD /VCR and home stereo repair for the Jamestown area that will also be able to eventually provide satellite TV installation/servicing and new electronics sales, making it the local leader in comprehensive electronic sales/services.

The company will be a sole proprietorship registered in the state of Jamestown and owned by Mr. Sammy Jay. The firm will have facilities on 530 Jamestown. The initial facilities will contain a sales area, repair room in the back of the shop, office space and storage for parts and equipment. The company is seeking a loan in order to finance the start up cost for operating the company. The owners will be putting up additional capital of their own as equity.

2.1 Start-up Summary

The data obtained for the start-up table comes from research done in the Jamestown area with other small electronics shops that have started their own business, in addition to Mr. Jay's previous experience within the industry. Inflation has been taken into account between the estimates of these fellow business owners (and when they started) and the current prices for expensed items. Much of the equipment to go into the facilities such as tools, are currently owned by Mr. Jay.

START UP FUNDING

Start-up Expenses to Fund	$26,300
Start-up Assets to Fund	$51,200
Total Funding Required	**$77,500**
Assets	
Non-cash Assets from Start-up	£15,000
Cash Requirements from Start-up	$36,200
Additional Cash Raised	$0
Cash Balance on Starting Date	$36,200
Total Assets	$51,200
Liabilities and Capital	
Liabilities	
Current Borrowing	$0
Long-term Liabilities	$15,400
Accounts Payable (Outstanding Bills)	$0
Other Current Liabilities (interest-free)	$13,600
Total Liabilities	$29,000
Planned Investment	
Sammy Jay	$26,500
Juliet Jay	$22,000
Additional Investment Requirement	$0
Total Planned Investment	$48,500
Loss at Start-up (Start-up Expenses)	($26,300)
Total Capital	$22,200
Total Capital and Liabilities	**$51,200**
Total Funding	***$77,500***

START UP

Requirements

Start-up Expenses

Legal	$500
Stationery etc.	$200
Advertising	$10,000
Phone	$200
Insurance	$400
Rent	$4,000
Utilities	$400
Facilities refurbishment	$8,000
Computer	$2,000
Other	$600
Total Start-up Expenses	**$26,300**
Start-up Assets	
Cash Required	$36,200
Start-up Inventory	$3,000
Other Current Assets	$8,000
Long-term Assets	$4,000
Total Assets	**$51,200**
Total Requirements	**$77,500**

Products and Services

Tesco Electronics offers a wide range of services as outlined in the detailed sections below. It is ultimately the goal of the company to offer a one-stop facility for all home entertainment needs, including both sales and servicing. This way the company can offer greater perceived value for the customer than many other shops which only offer sales or services.

The industry is highly competitive with suppliers having a great deal of power in setting and negotiating the prices of their products and services to repair shops. In addition, because the customers see the service as undifferentiated and a "commodity" with little value separation between competitors, buyer power is also very high. Finally, the barriers to entry are moderately low, and the large number of competitors in this field, including substitutes (such as do-it-yourself work) means that the pricing for such services is very competitive.

The only way to have an advantage in this industry is a low cost leadership principal applied aggressively or to create higher switching costs through the building of strong business-to-customer ties. It is the aim of Tesco Electronics to create a competitive advantage through both low cost strategy and offering greater value through its broader product and service line. Tesco Electronics will initially have only one factory trained and certified technician in the person of Mr. Jay. As the company grows and expands, Mr. Jay will hire trained and certified technicians who are able to prove they have superior customer awareness and interaction.

It is the company's professional people who will fulfill the firm's contracts and goals. The largest part of the company's expenses will be labor costs.

3.1 Product and Service Description

Tesco Electronics provides a wide range of home entertainment repair services. These include:

- Repair and cleaning of home and car stereos and CB radios.
- Repair and cleaning of TVs.
- Repair and cleaning of VCRs and DVDs.
- Sale of used TVs, stereos, VCRs and DVDs.
- Free estimates on repair jobs.

- Authorized warranty servicing on all major brands of home entertainment systems.
- House calls and free pickup and delivery.

Future products and services that Tesco Electronics will prepare to institute include TV/VCR/DVD rental, satellite TV installation and servicing, sales of new TVs, DVDs, VCRs and stereos, and repair/sale of microwave ovens. Mr. Jay is also investigating the possibility of offering a new product line of home entertainment cabinets in the near future.

3.2 Sourcing

Tesco Electronics will be obtaining most of its parts through established dealers and directly through the manufacturers of the relevant electronics. As part of the company's low cost strategy, the company will seek to purchase parts in large quantities whenever possible to take advantage of volume discounts. In addition, the company will aggressively seek to procure its parts from local suppliers in order to start forming close relations with such companies. It is the ultimate aim of Tesco Electronics to form strategic partnerships with such companies in order to lower overall costs of parts. A large part of Tesco Electronics enhanced services will be free pickup and delivery of electronics to a person's home.

Mr. Jay's cousin, Mr. Stephen Biss, owns Caesar Courier Services, a local company providing pickup and delivery services. Mr. Biss has agreed to provide these services to Tesco Electronics' clients at discounted prices to Mr. Jay.

3.3 Technology

The technological revolution in computers has enhanced our abilities to diagnose and repair our clients' home electronics. Tesco Electronics will remain on the cutting edge by instituting the use of computer diagnostic equipment in its shop.

The company will continue to seek new ways to provide a better service through technology.

3.4 Competitive Comparison

The electronics repair industry is highly competitive. Each company within this field has high labor costs, low margins, and a high intensity of competition.

Suppliers have a great deal of power in setting and negotiating the prices of their products and services to repair shops. This is due to the fact that the suppliers who absorb the greatest amounts of cash from repair shops are large electronic manufacturing companies such as Panasonic, Emerson, Toshiba, etc. These companies are more consolidated than the repair industry, have deeper pockets, an almost limitless number of substitute customers, and finally they are the single most important supplier to the electronic repair industry. Therefore, these companies can set whatever price they wish to. Furthermore, labor is the single most important expense in this industry, and salaries for such individuals are well known and not very flexible.

In addition, because the customers see the service as undifferentiated and a "commodity" with little value separation between competitors (if they offer a suitable level of quality) buyer power is also very high. Additionally, the costs of our services are not cheap, and buyers are willing to search for the most favorable combination of price and acceptable service. The barriers to entry and exit are moderately low in this industry. Switching costs are virtually non-existent and the costs to entry and exist the market are low. The large number of competitors in this field including substitutes means that pricing for such services are very competitive. The only way to have an advantage in this industry is a low cost leadership principal applied aggressively to all aspects of the business or to build up customer relations to a point where the switching costs are raised. Based on this analysis, Tesco Electronics will pursue a low cost leadership strategy as its primary competitive advantage.

Furthermore, the company will simultaneously build up its product and service line to take advantage of the limited opportunity to create higher switching costs through enhanced value creation and through cost spreading.

3.5 Future Products and Services

Future products and services that Tesco Electronics will prepare to institute include TV/VCR/DVD rental, satellite TV installation and servicing, sales of new TVs, DVDs VCRs and stereos, and repair /sale of microwave ovens. Mr. Jay is also investigating the possibility of offering a new product line of home entertainment cabinets at in the near future.

Tesco Electronics will start implementing these new products or services in the following time periods:

- Repair/sale of microwave ovens (3rd Qtr 2004).
- Satellite TV installation and servicing (3rd Qtr 2005).
- TV/VCR/DVD rental (2nd Qtr 2006).
- Sales of new TVs/DVDs/VCRs (4th Qtr 2006).

The capital investment needed for such expansion will primarily come from the company's accumulated operating cash account. It is anticipated that some of these product/service expansions that require significant inventory, such as new sales, may require additional cash inflow such as loans. The company will be preparing proposals for various lending institutions in anticipation of this need.

Presently the product that is really driving the electronics repair market is computers. While Tesco Electronics is not currently positioned to take advantage of this situation, it is the long-term goal of Tesco electronics to incorporate computer repair services within the company. Once the firm is able to generate enough cash to retain the services of a computer repair technician, the company will evaluate the viability of such a move.

It is anticipated that this service will be offered sometime after 1st Qtr 2007.

Market Analysis Summary

There are approximately 332,500 households in the greater Jamestown area, which includes suburbs such as Nima, Osu, and South Jamestown. Virtually all of these households have TVs, VCRs, etc. Tesco Electronics segments its market into product categories that reflect the estimated number of each electronic device currently being used in the greater Jamestown area, since each of these devices may fail at any time and require our services. In addition the growth rate of each product emplaced in the home is based on the current sales growth of each product. Presently, the fastest growing product, in terms of sales, is the DVD player. It is anticipated that the DVD will replace the VCR within the next three to five years as movie rental stores replace their existing VHS movies with DVD. The largest segment is the home and car stereo segment, since usually a household has more than one of these systems. The company will be focusing on servicing all of these systems, and not focusing on one over the other.

4.1 Market Segmentation

Tesco Electronics has segmented the households in the Jamestown area as follows:

- Couples with children.
- Couples without children (including Baby Boomers).
- Retired people.
- Students living in multi-unit housing.
- Single people living alone.
- Single people living with roommates.

Tesco will target the following segments:

Middle class couples without children. This group will tend to have a higher disposable income since they have two incomes but do not have the expense of children. They prioritize socializing and spend a fair amount of time entertaining in their home and in the homes of their friends. For this reason they will spend more on their electronic equipment.

Single men living alone or with roommates This group is not the largest segment for us, but potentially one of the most profitable, since single men tend to prioritize their home entertainment equipment. They will spend a greater percentage of their income on high-quality TV and stereo equipment.

Baby boomers Are reaching the age where their children have left home and they have more disposable income than when their children were young and living at home. They are more tech savvy than the generation before them and appreciate the good things in life. They like to spend time in their homes, now that the children are out of the house.

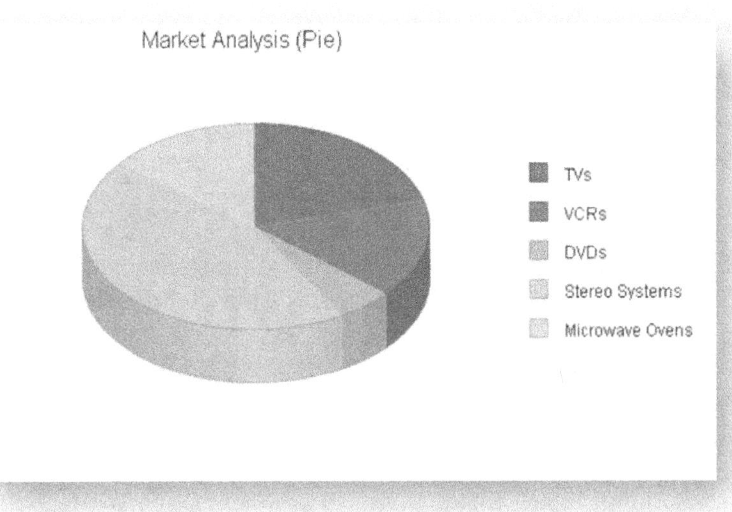

Market Analysis

Potential Customers	Growth	Year 1	Year 2	Year 3	Year 4	Year 5	CAGR
TVs	3%	415,875	428,351	441,202	454,438	468,071	3.00%
VCRs	-2%	310,645	304,432	298,343	292,376	286,528	-2.00%
DVDs	25%	106,400	133,000	166,250	207,813	259,766	25.00%
Stereo Systems	12%	875,500	980,560	1,098,227	1,230,014	1,377,616	12.00%
Microwave Ovens	8%	282,625	305,235	329,654	356,026	384,508	8.00%
Total	8.67%	1,991,045	2,151,578	2,333,676	2,540,667	2,776,489	8.67%

4.1.1 Market Trends

The market demand for electronics repair has been relatively stable over the past decade. With the advent of DVD players, the market is seeing more highly trained technicians needed. As technology progresses, long-term planners within this market expect to see new opportunities for electronics repair quickly arise. Such devices as cellular telephones, PDAs and other new electronics may have a role to play in the people who have a broad vision in this field.

4.2 Service Business Analysis

Much of the electronics repair industry analysis is contained in the competitive comparison section. However, the key points are that the industry is highly competitive and that most firms have little power to affect the forces that influence them or to affect the price levels that the market determines. In essence, Tesco Electronics operates in a purely competitive environment where the demand curve is horizontal. In other words the company is free to service electronics at maximum capacity without effecting the price or demand for its services.

With this type of environment and with customers seeing such services as a "commodity" the only strategy open to companies in this field is the low cost leadership approach.Tesco Electronics is fortunate in that Juliet Jay, Mr. Jay's wife works in cost analysis for Sony, one of the country's best low cost companies. Mrs. Jay has agreed to furnish cost analysis services to Tesco Electronics for free. The low cost leadership strategy will not be simple to achieve. Realistically speaking, because of the fragmented nature of the industry, Tesco Electronics will only seek a low cost leadership in the Jamestown region for the first seven to ten years of operations.

In order to capture this position and achieve its benefits of high market share and profitability, the company is expected to have higher start-up costs and lower profits within the first few years as the company invests in better and more efficient facilities and equipment than most competitors and engages in aggressive pricing to capture market share.

The company will rigorously evaluate every aspect of the company to improve efficiency and lower costs. Mrs. Jay is preparing an analysis of the company's value chain and cost drivers to identify where costs can be lowered and which aspects of the business Mr. Jay must focus on. It is expected that management will expend a great deal of energy in cost management and the reduction of things such as marginal customer accounts and marketing expenses. Once in operation, management will concentrate on developing established procedures that will create the most effective service experience. Finally, as part of this low cost leadership strategy, the company plans to vertically integrate to include original sales and broad services that will spread costs and serve all major customer types so as to build volume.

4.2.1 Competition and Buying Patterns

Customers traditionally purchase services in this industry based on effective advertising and reputation. The customers wish to be reassured that they will receive a prompt and reliable service, coupled with an understanding that our service representative will listen to their problems and seek to solve them in a fast and professional manner.
Therefore image during the entire service experience is crucial to maintain word-of-mouth marketing to keep cost down. Currently the largest problem that faces small firms is product/service awareness. By the use of effective and widespread advertising, Tesco Electronics expects to be able to capitalize on the weakness of the "mom and pop" outfits' style of passive promotion (such as Yellow Page ads) and to leverage greater product awareness into higher market share. There is no seasonality to this industry although there is some slight increase in servicing sales during the Christmas season.

4.2.2 Business Participants

As stated before, the electronic repair industry is highly fragmented. In fact, there are so many small providers that any company in this industry is facing a purely competitive environment. Approximately 23,700 electronic repair firms exist in the country today. Firms within this field range in sizes from the "mom and pop" outfits such as Sam's Electronics and Phil Repair in downtown Jamestown to regional companies like Hitata Hi-Fi and the national chains. Not all of these firms are purely repair outfits. In fact all of the larger firmsmake the majority of their revenue in original sales. It is these companies that have the largest market share and have the opportunity to compete by differentiating on customer service or product/service range.

As stated before, Tesco Electronics will seek a low cost leadership approach in the local Jamestown region first. Its goals are not to directly compete with the larger companies who could effectively out compete Tesco Electronics. Instead, the company will seek to out price the local "mom and pop" outfits and acquire their market share in order to then compete with the regional firms. There are eight such "mom & pop" firms that will be Tesco Electronics' main competitors in its first few years of operation.

They are:

- Sam's Electronics.
- Phil Repair.
- Cactus Repair and Appliance.
- Ait TV.
- Billy's Repair.
- Sam the TV Man.
- Thelma Service Co.
- Frederick TV Shoppe.

Strategy and Implementation Summary

The following sections outline Tesco Electronics' strategy and implementation summary.

5.1 Marketing Strategy

The company has a strong program for marketing its services that include the following:

1. Flyers
2. Direct mailers
3. Discounts
4. Newspaper ads
5. Yellow Pages
6. Referrals through other local businesses
7. Radio ads
8. Billboards
9. Web banners on local information sites

The company's aim is to overcome the traditional small firm's passive form of advertising and promotion by sending our message to the customer, instead of having the customer look for a firm when they need our services.

The share development graph below shows how the company plans to build market share through service awareness, value creation, competitive price, availability, and attractive service experience, all leading to the purchasing of our services. The numbers given in the graph give the estimated percentages of those customers who respond favorably to each marketing step. These numbers multiplied together give us an estimated aggregate market share of approximately 16%. The company expects to achieve this by year four.

5.1.1 Pricing Strategy

Tesco Electronics exists in a purely competitive environment where each firm must be a price taker. In other words, the firm has no ability to affect the market price of its services, regardless of how many TVs/DVDs or VCRs it repairs. In this case, therefore, marginal revenue (the revenue incurred by producing or servicing one more unit) is equal to the price charged. Furthermore, because the demand curve is essentially horizontal, Tucson Electronics can service electronics at total capacity without affecting the price.

What all of this means for the company is that we must seek to charge our clients at the market price (or lower). Research has shown that the average price is approximately £75 per electronic device. As long as marginal costs do not exceed revenues, the company's method to maximize short-run profits is to service the various electronic devices at maximum capacity. This means that Tesco Electronics (TE) can expect a long-term ROA of approximately 14%.

5.1.2 Promotion Strategy

The company's promotion strategy will take the form of flyers, direct mailers, price discounts, billboards, radio ads and advertisements in newspapers and yellow pages. TE expects to spend a large amount on marketing in the first two years in order to build up product awareness and service value in the minds of our customers.

5.2 Competitive Edge

Tesco Electronics' competitive edge lies in its ability to provide quality and fast electronic repair at lower cost than any local small competitor. This positioning of the company provides protection against the power of suppliers by creating more flexibility to cope with increasing costs.

In addition, this approach will provide returns even during economic downturns and when other unforeseen problems arise.

Sales Forecast

Since the electronic repair industry is, operationally, a job-shop environment, it is somewhat difficult to estimate sales. For job-shops, each individual product or service is tailored or unique to that job, and is only initiated once an order is made. However, the sales forecast reflect the professional opinion of Mr. Jay in how many sales he will make.

The sales forecast is based on the estimated number of electronics the company could service that are currently emplaced in the homes in Jamestown. This is conservatively estimated at about two million units. From that number it is assumed that approximately 3% of all those will fail in any year. These two numbers multiplied together give us yearly market demand for our services. With an aggressive promotional strategy, a 10% market share is assumed by year three and multiplied by the estimated market demand.

This is then multiplied by the estimated price per unit to arrive at the yearly sales figure assumed for year three (once the company's marketing efforts have paid off). This number is then decreased by a logical amount to estimate the first two years of revenue.

Sales Monthly
$24,000
$21,000
$18,000
$15,000
$12,000
$9,000
$6,000
$3,000
$0
Month 1
Month 2
Month 3
Month 4
Month 5
Month 6
Month 7
Month 8
Month 9
Month 10
Month 11
Month 12
TVs
VCRs
DVDs
Stereo Systems
Microwave Ovens

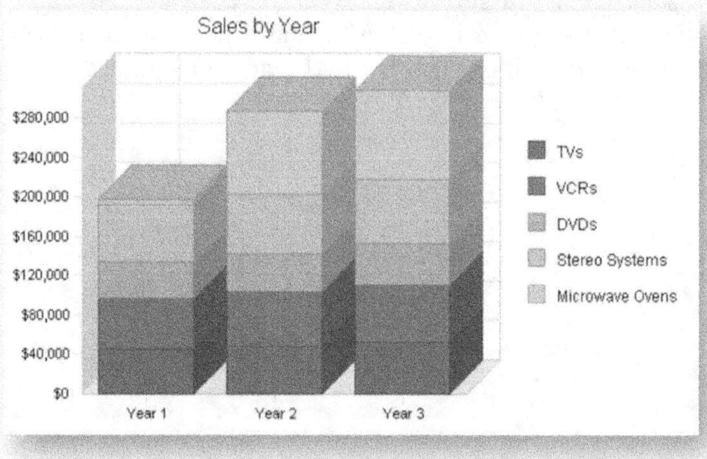

Sales by Year
$280,000
$240,000
$200,000
$160,000
$120,000
$80,000
$40,000
$0
Year 1
Year 2
Year 3
TVs
VCRs
DVDs
Stereo Systems
Microwave Ovens

Sales Forecast

	Year 1	Year 2	Year 3
Sales			
TVs	$46,250	$49,025	$52,604
VCRs	$51,600	$54,696	$58,689
DVDs	$36,500	$38,690	$41,514
Stereo Systems	$57,700	$61,162	$65,627
Microwave Ovens	$5,900	$84,000	$90,132
Total Sales	**$197,950**	**$287,573**	**$308,566**
Direct Cost of Sales	Year 1	Year 2	Year 3
TVs	$4,625	$6,000	$6,000
VCRs	$5,160	$7,200	$7,200
DVDs	$3,650	$8,400	$8,400
Stereo Systems	$5,770	$7,200	$7,200
Microwave Ovens	$590	$7,200	$7,200
Subtotal Direct Cost of Sales	**$19,795**	**$36,000**	**$36,000**

Management Summary

Mr. Sammy Jay is a retired Electrical Engineer with a degree in electrical engineering from the University of Technology. During his career, Mr. Jay gained extensive experience in project management, engineering, and electronics systems. During his leisure time, Mr. Jay sought to expand his experiences in electronics by becoming a certified electronics technician with various brand companies. Mr. Jay is now seeking to leverage this experience into a growth-oriented business that will be able to eventually compete with the largest firms in the industry. Mr. Jay will also be employing the services of his son Victor, who desires to eventually take over the business. Victor Jay has been attending a local trade school and is expected to graduate with a degree in electronics in the summer of 2002.

7.1 Personnel Plan

Tesco Electronics' initial staffing will consist of Mr. Jay, his son, and two part-time technician trainees. Accounting, bookkeeping, and marketing consulting services will be outsourced. The company's intermediate goal is to have four full-time, fully trained technicians at the original facility, plus a full-time office manager. However, management has decided to await future developments before determining the best time to bring on such personnel.

Payroll Plan	Year 1	Year 2	Year 3
Mr. Sammy Jay	$36,000	$36,000	$36,000
Mr. Victor Jay	$24,000	$28,000	$32,000
Part-time technician	$14,400	$28,000	$28,000
Part-time technician	$14,400	$28,000	$28,000
Part-time technician	$0	$15,000	$15,000
Total People	4	5	5
Total Payroll	**£88,800**	**£135,000**	**£139,000**

Financial Plan

The following sections outline the financial plan for Tesco Electroni-incs.

General Assumptions

	Year 1	Year 2	Year 3
Plan Month	1	2	3
Current Interest Rate	10.00%	10.00%	10.00%
Long-term Interest Rate	10.00%	10.00%	10.00%
Tax Rate	30.00%	30.00%	30.00%
Other	0	0	0

8.1 Break-even Analysis

The company's break-even analysis is based on an average company's running costs within this industry, including payroll, and its fixed costs for such things as rent, utilities, etc.

As Tesco Electronics operates as a job-shop, with each task a unique, customized service, it is difficult to estimate revenue per unit and variable costs. The reader must understand that there is a high degree of variance within these estimates. The reader will also note that the company is not expected to reach its break-even point until the last three months of sales of the first year.

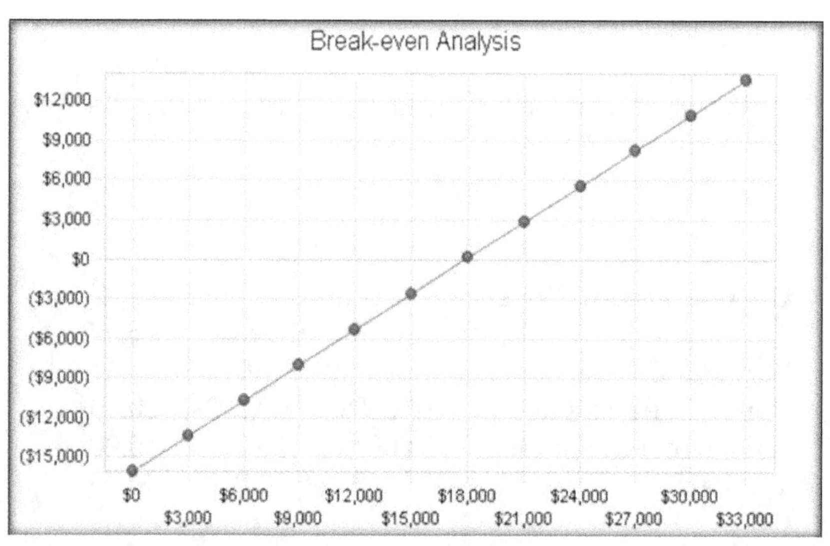

Break-even Analysis

Monthly Revenue Break-even $17,844

Assumptions:

Average Percent Variable Cost   10%

Estimated Monthly Fixed Cost $16,059

8.2 Projected Profit and Loss

The following table and charts are the projected profit and loss for Tesco Electronics.

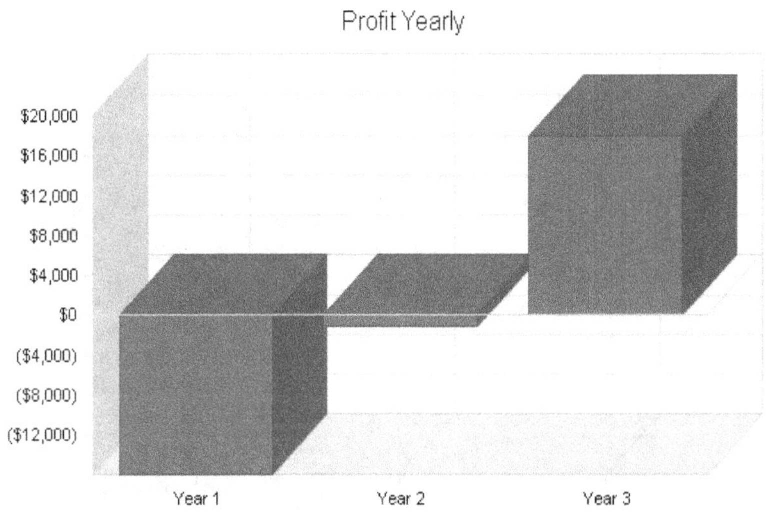

Gross Margin Monthly

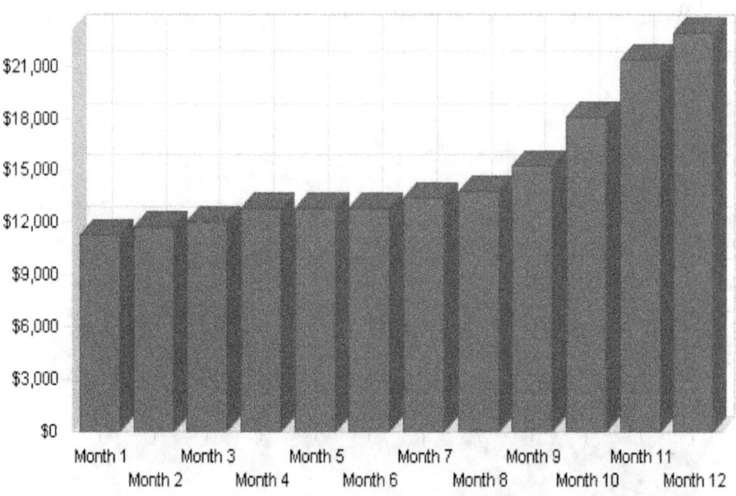

Gross Margin Yearly

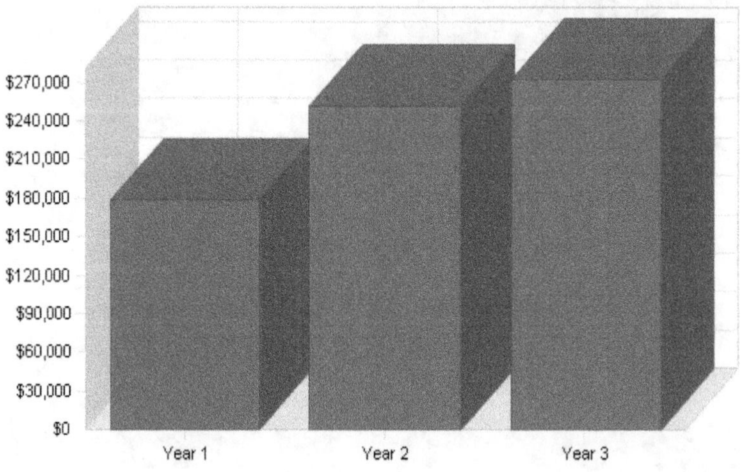

Profit Monthly

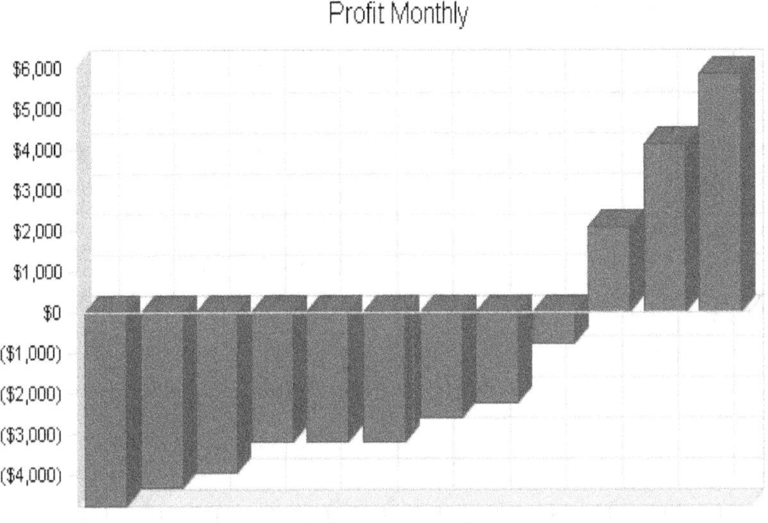

Pro Forma Profit and Loss

	Year 1	Year 2	Year 3
Sales	$197,950	$287,573	$308,566
Direct Cost of Sales	$19,795	$36,000	$36,000
Other Production Expenses	$0	$0	$0
Total Cost of Sales	**$19,795**	**$36,000**	**$36,000**
Gross Margin	$178,155	$251,573	$272,566
Gross Margin %	90.00%	87.48%	88.33%
Expenses			
Payroll	$88,800	$135,000	$139,000
Sales and Marketing and Other Expenses	$28,600	$36,000	$26,000
Depreciation	$1,992	$2,000	$2,000
Leased Equipment	$6,000	$2,000	$2,000
Utilities	$4,800	$5,000	$5,000
Insurance	$7,200	$7,400	$7,400
Rent	$42,000	$44,000	$44,000
Payroll Taxes	$13,320	$20,250	$20,850
Other	$0	$0	$0
Total Operating Expenses	**$192,712**	**$251,650**	**$246,250**
Profit Before Interest and Taxes	($14,557)	($77)	$26,316
EBITDA	($12,565)	$1,923	$28,316
Interest Expense	$1,370	$1,000	$640
Taxes Incurred	$0	$0	$7,703
Net Profit	**($15,927)**	**($1,077)**	**$17,973**
Net Profit/Sales	**-8.05%**	**-0.37%**	**5.82%**

8.3 Projected Cash Flow

The following chart and table is the projected cash flow for Tesco Electronics.

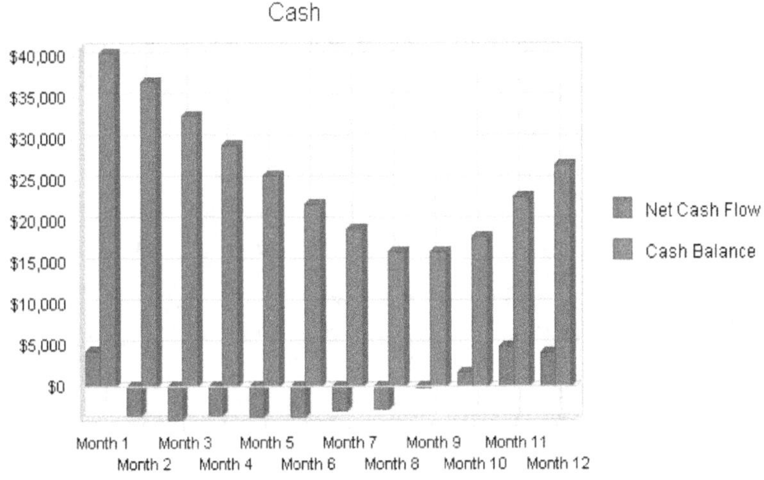

Pro Forma Cash Flow

	Year 1	Year 2	Year 3
Cash Received			
Cash from Operations			
Cash Sales	$197,950	$287,573	$308,566
Subtotal Cash from Operations	**$197,950**	**$287,573**	**$308,566**
Additional Cash Received			
Sales Tax, VAT, HST/GST Received	$0	$0	$0
New Current Borrowing	$1,000	$0	$0
New Other Liabilities (interest-free)	$0	$0	$0
New Long-term Liabilities	$0	$0	$0
Sales of Other Current Assets	$0	$0	$0
Sales of Long-term Assets	$0	$0	$0
New Investment Received	$0	$3,000	$0
Subtotal Cash Received	$198,950	$290,573	$308,566
Expenditures	Year 1	Year 2	Year 3
Expenditures from Operations			
Cash Spending	$88,800	$135,000	$139,000
Bill Payments	$111,148	$153,016	$149,950
Subtotal Spent on Operations	**$199,948**	**$288,016**	**$288,950**
Additional Cash Spent			
Sales Tax, VAT, HST/GST Paid Out	$0	$0	$0
Principal Repayment of Current Borrowing	$1,000	$0	$0
Other Liabilities Principal Repayment	$3,600	$3,600	$3,600
Long-term Liabilities Principal Repayment	$3,600	$3,600	$3,600
Purchase Other Current Assets	$0	$2,000	$3,000
Purchase Long-term Assets	$0	$5,000	$5,000
Dividends	$0	$0	$0
Subtotal Cash Spent	**$208,148**	**$302,216**	**$304,150**
Net Cash Flow	**($9,198)**	**($11,643)**	**$4,416**
Cash Balance	**$27,002**	**$15,359**	**$19,775**

Pro Forma Balance Sheet

	Year 1	Year 2	Year 3
Assets			
Current Assets			
Cash	$27,002	$15,359	$19,775
Inventory	$2,794	$5,081	$5,081
Other Current Assets	$8,000	$10,000	$13,000
Total Current Assets	**$37,796**	**$30,440**	**$37,856**
Long-term Assets			
Long-term Assets	$4,000	$9,000	$14,000
Accumulated Depreciation	$1,992	$3,992	$5,992
Total Long-term Assets	$2,008	$5,008	$8,008
Total Assets	**$39,804**	**$35,448**	**$45,864**
Liabilities and Capital	Year 1	Year 2	Year 3
Current Liabilities			
Accounts Payable	$11,731	$12,652	$12,295
Current Borrowing	$0	$0	$0
Other Current Liabilities	$10,000	$6,400	$2,800
Subtotal Current Liabilities	$21,731	$19,052	$15,095
Long-term Liabilities	$11,800	$8,200	$4,600
Total Liabilities	**$33,531**	**$27,252**	**$19,695**
Paid-in Capital	$48,500	$51,500	$51,500
Retained Earnings	($26,300)	($42,227)	($43,304)
Earnings	($15,927)	($1,077)	$17,973
Total Capital	**$6,273**	**$8,196**	**$26,169**
Total Liabilities and Capital	***$39,804***	***$35,448***	***$45,864***
Net Worth	**$6,273**	**$8,196**	**$26,169**

8.5 Business Ratios

The Business ratios give an overall idea of how profitable, and at what risk level, Tesco Electronics will operate at. The ratio table gives both time series analysis and cross-sectional analysis by including industry average ratios. Industry Profile ratios are based on Standard Industrial Classification (SIC) code 7622, Radio and Television Repair. As can be seen from the comparison between industry standards and Tesco Electronics own ratios, there are some differences. Most of these are due to the fact that there is a very large variance in assets, liabilities, financing, and net income between companies in this industry due to the vast differences in company size.

The reader will also note that there is a fair amount of variability between the various years. This is due to the fact that the company is expected to grow quickly and have a large variance in profitability from year to year at first. Overall the company's projections show a company that faces the usual risks of companies in this industry and one that will be profitable in the long-run. The company shows that it has higher advertising and start-up costs than othercompetitors; however management has deliberately overstated costs and minimized profits in order to create a "safe" or "buffer" zone in case of hard times or other unforeseeable problems.

Pre-tax return on net worth and pre-tax return on assets appears to be very high, especially within the first two years, however again this is due to the fact that the company will be facing highly variable revenue and costs over the first few years.

	Year 1	Year 2	Year 3	Industry Profile
Sales Growth	0.00%	45.28%	7.30%	6.10%
Percent of Total Assets				
Inventory	7.02%	14.33%	11.08%	19.00%
Other Current Assets	20.10%	28.21%	28.34%	27.50%
Total Current Assets	94.96%	85.87%	82.54%	76.90%
Long-term Assets	5.04%	14.13%	17.46%	23.10%
Total Assets	**100.00%**	**100.00%**	**100.00%**	**100.00%**
Current Liabilities	54.59%	53.75%	32.91%	36.90%
Long-term Liabilities	29.65%	23.13%	10.03%	15.80%
Total Liabilities	**84.24%**	**76.88%**	**42.94%**	**52.70%**
Net Worth	**15.76%**	**23.12%**	**57.06%**	**47.30%**
Percent of Sales				
Sales	100.00%	100.00%	100.00%	100.00%
Gross Margin	90.00%	87.48%	88.33%	0.00%
Selling, General & Administrative Expenses	97.70%	87.54%	82.32%	83.50%
Advertising Expenses	7.07%	8.69%	4.86%	0.50%
Profit Before Interest and Taxes	-7.35%	-0.03%	8.53%	3.10%
Main Ratios				
Current	1.74	1.60	2.51	2.26
Quick	1.61	1.33	2.17	1.47
Total Debt to Total Assets	84.24%	76.88%	42.94%	52.70%
Pre-tax Return on Net Worth	-253.90%	-13.14%	98.12%	7.00%
Pre-tax Return on Assets	-40.01%	-3.04%	55.98%	14.70%
Additional Ratios	Year 1	Year 2	Year 3	
Net Profit Margin	-8.05%	-0.37%	5.82%	n.a
Return on Equity	-253.90%	-13.14%	68.68%	n.a
Activity Ratios				
Inventory Turnover	10.71	9.14	7.08	n.a
Accounts Payable Turnover	10.47	12.17	12.17	n.a
Payment Days	27	29	30	n.a
Total Asset Turnover	**4.97**	**8.11**	**6.73**	**n.a**
Debt Ratios				
Debt to Net Worth	5.35	3.33	0.75	n.a
Current Liab. to Liab.	0.65	0.70	0.77	n.a
Liquidity Ratios				
Net Working Capital	$16,065	$11,388	$22,761	n.a
Interest Coverage	-10.63	-0.08	41.12	n.a
Additional Ratios				
Assets to Sales	0.20	0.12	0.15	n.a
Current Debt/Total Assets	55%	54%	33%	n.a
Acid Test	1.61	1.33	2.17	n.a
Sales/Net Worth	**31.56**	**35.09**	**11.79**	**n.a**
Dividend Payout	0.00	0.00	0.00	n.a

Sales Forecast

		Mth 1	Mth 2	Mth 3	Mth 4	Mth 5	Mth 6	Mth 7	Mth 8	Mth 9	Mth 10	Mth 11	Mth 12
Sales													
TVs	0%	$3,000	$3,200	$3,400	$3,550	$3,550	$3,550	$3,700	$3,700	$4,000	$4,800	$4,800	$5,000
VCRs	0%	$3,500	$3,600	$3,700	$3,900	$3,900	$3,900	$4,000	$4,200	$4,500	$5,100	$5,400	$5,900
DVDs	0%	$2,000	$2,200	$2,200	$2,400	$2,400	$2,400	$2,600	$2,600	$3,000	$4,200	$5,000	$5,500
Stereo Systems	0%	$4,000	$4,000	$4,100	$4,400	$4,400	$4,400	$4,600	$4,800	$5,400	$5,600	$6,000	$6,000
Microwave Ovens	0%	$0	$0	$0	$0	$0	$0	$0	$0	$0	$400	$2,500	$3,000
Total Sales		$12,500	$13,000	$13,400	$14,250	$14,250	$14,250	$14,900	$15,300	$16,900	$20,100	$23,700	$25,400

	Mth 1	Mth 2	Mth 3	Mth 4	Mth 5	Mth 6	Mth 7	Mth 8	Mth 9	Mth 10	Mth 11	Mth 12
Direct Cost of Sales												
TVs	$300	$320	$340	$355	$355	$355	$370	$370	$400	$480	$480	$500
VCRs	$350	$360	$370	$390	$390	$390	$400	$420	$450	$510	$540	$590
DVDs	$200	$220	$220	$240	$240	$240	$260	$260	$300	$420	$500	$550
Stereo Systems	$400	$400	$410	$440	$440	$440	$460	$480	$540	$560	$600	$600
Microwave Ovens	$0	$0	$0	$0	$0	$0	$0	$0	$0	$40	$250	$300
Subtotal Direct Cost of Sales	$1,250	$1,300	$1,340	$1,425	$1,425	$1,425	$1,490	$1,530	$1,690	$2,010	$2,370	$2,540

Personnel Plan		Mth 1	Mth 2	Mth 3	Mth 4	Mth 5	Mth 6	Mth 7	Mth 8	Mth 9	Mth 10	Mth 11	Mth 12
Mr. Sammy Jay	0%	$3,000	$3,000	$3,000	$3,000	$3,000	$3,000	$3,000	$3,000	$3,000	$3,000	$3,000	$3,000
Mr. Victor Jay	0%	$2,000	$2,000	$2,000	$2,000	$2,000	$2,000	$2,000	$2,000	$2,000	$2,000	$2,000	$2,000
Part-time technician	0%	$1,200	$1,200	$1,200	$1,200	$1,200	$1,200	$1,200	$1,200	$1,200	$1,200	$1,200	$1,200
Part-time technician	0%	$1,200	$1,200	$1,200	$1,200	$1,200	$1,200	$1,200	$1,200	$1,200	$1,200	$1,200	$1,200
Part-time technician	0%	$0	$0	$0	$0	$0	$0	$0	$0	$0	$0	$0	$0
Total People		4	4	4	4	4	4	4	4	4	4	4	4
Total Payroll		$7,400	$7,400	$7,400	$7,400	$7,400	$7,400	$7,400	$7,400	$7,400	$7,400	$7,400	$7,400

General Assumptions

	Mth 1	Mth 2	Mth 3	Mth 4	Mth 5	Mth 6	Mth 7	Mth 8	Mth 9	Mth 10	Mth 11	Mth 12
Plan Mth	1	2	3	4	5	6	7	8	9	10	11	12
Current Interest Rate	10%	10%	10%	10%	10%	10%	10%	10%	10%	10%	10%	10%
Long-term Interest Rate	10%	10%	10%	10%	10%	10%	10%	10%	10%	10%	10%	10%
Tax Rate	30%	30%	30%	30%	30%	30%	30%	30%	30%	30%	30%	30%
Other	0	0	0	0	0	0	0	0	0	0	0	0

Additional Double Page Forecasts

PRO FORMA PROFIT AND LOSS	Mth 1	Mth 2	Mth 3	Mth 4
Sales	$12,500	$13,000	$13,400	$14,250
Direct Cost of Sales	$1,250	$1,300	$1,340	$1,425
Other Production Expense	$0	$0	$0	$0
Total Cost of Sales	**$1,250**	**$1,300**	**$1,340**	**$1,425**
Gross Margin	$11,250	$11,700	$12,060	$12,825
Gross Margin %	90.00%	90.00%	90.00%	90.00%
Expenses				
Payroll	$7,400	$7,400	$7,400	$7,400
Sales and Marketing and Other Expenses	$2,200	$2,200	$2,200	$2,200
Depreciation	$166	$166	$166	$166
Leased Equipment	$500	$500	$500	$500
Utilities	$400	$400	$400	$400
Insurance	$600	$600	$600	$600
Rent	$3,500	$3,500	$3,500	$3,500
Payroll Taxes 15%	$1,110	$1,110	$1,110	$1,110
Other	$0	$0	$0	$0
Total Operating Expenses	**$15,876**	**$15,876**	**$15,876**	**$15,876**
Profit Before Interest and Taxes	($4,626)	($4,176)	($3,816)	($3,051)
EBITDA	($4,460)	($4,010)	($3,650)	($2,885)
Interest Expense	$126	$123	$121	$118
Taxes Incurred	$0	$0	$0	$0
Net Profit	**($4,752)**	**($4,299)**	**($3,937)**	**($3,169)**
Net Profit/Sales	**-38.01%**	**-33.07%**	**-29.38%**	**-22.24%**

Mth 5	Mth 6	Mth 7	Mth 8	Mth 9	Mth 10	Mth 11	Mth 12
$14,250	$14,250	$14,900	$15,300	$16,900	$20,100	$23,700	$25,400
$1,425	$1,425	$1,490	$1,530	$1,690	$2,010	$2,370	$2,540
$0	$0	$0	$0	$0	$0	$0	$0
$1,425	**$1,425**	**$1,490**	**$1,530**	**$1,690**	**$2,010**	**$2,370**	**$2,540**
$12,825	$12,825	$13,410	$13,770	$15,210	$18,090	$21,330	$22,860
90.00%	90.00%	90.00%	90.00%	90.00%	90.00%	90.00%	90.00%
$7,400	$7,400	$7,400	$7,400	$7,400	$7,400	$7,400	$7,400
$2,200	$2,200	$2,200	$2,200	$2,200	$2,200	$3,400	$3,200
$166	$166	$166	$166	$166	$166	$166	$166
$500	$500	$500	$500	$500	$500	$500	$500
$400	$400	$400	$400	$400	$400	$400	$400
$600	$600	$600	$600	$600	$600	$600	$600
$3,500	$3,500	$3,500	$3,500	$3,500	$3,500	$3,500	$3,500
$1,110	$1,110	$1,110	$1,110	$1,110	$1,110	$1,110	$1,110
$0	$0	$0	$0	$0	$0	$0	$0
$15,876	**$15,876**	**$15,876**	**$15,876**	**$15,876**	**$15,876**	**$17,076**	**$16,876**
($3,051)	($3,051)	($2,466)	($2,106)	($666)	$2,214	$4,254	$5,984
($2,885)	($2,885)	($2,300)	($1,940)	($500)	$2,380	$4,420	$6,150
$116	$113	$111	$108	$114	$112	$109	$98
$0	$0	$0	$0	$0	$0	$0	$0
($3,167)	**($3,164)**	**($2,577)**	**($2,214)**	**($780)**	**$2,102**	**$4,145**	**$5,886**
-22.22%	**-22.21%**	**-17.29%**	**-14.47%**	**-4.62%**	**10.46%**	**17.49%**	**23.17%**

CASH FLOW	Mth 1	Mth 2	Mth 3	Mth 4
Cash Received from Operations				
Cash Sales	$12,500	$13,000	$13,400	$14,250
Subtotal Cash from Operations	**$12,500**	**$13,000**	**$13,400**	**$14,250**
Sales Tax, VAT, HST/GST Received 0%	$0	$0	$0	$0
New Current Borrowing	$0	$0	$0	$0
New Other Liabilities (interest-free)	$0	$0	$0	$0
New Long-term Liabilities	$0	$0	$0	$0
Sales of Other Current Assets	$0	$0	$0	$0
Sales of Long-term Assets	$0	$0	$0	$0
New Investment Received	$0	$0	$0	$0
Subtotal Cash Received	**$12,500**	**$13,000**	**$13,400**	**$14,250**
Expenditures from Operations				
Cash Spending	$7,400	$7,400	$7,400	$7,400
Bill Payments	$281	$8,469	$9,445	$9,800
Subtotal Spent on Operations	**$7,681**	**$15,869**	**$16,845**	**$17,200**
Sales Tax, VAT, HST/GST Paid Out	$0	$0	$0	$0
Principal Repayment of Current Borrowing	$0	$0	$0	$0
Other Liabilities Principal Repayment	$300	$300	$300	$300
Long-term Liabilities Principal Repayment	$300	$300	$300	$300
Purchase Other Current Assets	$0	$0	$0	$0
Purchase Long-term Assets	$0	$0	$0	$0
Dividends	$0	$0	$0	$0
Subtotal Cash Spent	**$8,281**	**$16,469**	**$17,445**	**$17,800**
Net Cash Flow	**$4,219**	**($3,469)**	**($4,045)**	**($3,550)**
Cash Balance	$40,419	$36,950	$32,904	$29,354

Mth 5	Mth 6	Mth 7	Mth 8	Mth 9	Mth 10	Mth 11	Mth 12
$14,250	$14,250	$14,900	$15,300	$16,900	$20,100	$23,700	$25,400
$14,250	**$14,250**	**$14,900**	**$15,300**	**$16,900**	**$20,100**	**$23,700**	**$25,400**
$0	$0	$0	$0	$0	$0	$0	$0
$0	$0	$0	$0	$1,000	$0	$0	$0
$0	$0	$0	$0	$0	$0	$0	$0
$0	$0	$0	$0	$0	$0	$0	$0
$0	$0	$0	$0	$0	$0	$0	$0
$0	$0	$0	$0	$0	$0	$0	$0
$0	$0	$0	$0	$0	$0	$0	$0
$14,250	**$14,250**	**$14,900**	**$15,300**	**$17,900**	**$20,100**	**$23,700**	**$25,400**
$7,400	$7,400	$7,400	$7,400	$7,400	$7,400	$7,400	$7,400
$9,944	$9,851	$9,853	$9,983	$10,002	$10,307	$10,837	$12,377
$17,344	$17,251	$17,253	$17,383	$17,402	$17,707	$18,237	$19,777
$0	$0	$0	$0	$0	$0	$0	$0
$0	$0	$0	$0	$0	$0	$0	$1,000
$300	$300	$300	$300	$300	$300	$300	$300
$300	$300	$300	$300	$300	$300	$300	$300
$0	$0	$0	$0	$0	$0	$0	$0
$0	$0	$0	$0	$0	$0	$0	$0
$0	$0	$0	$0	$0	$0	$0	$0
$17,944	**$17,851**	**$17,853**	**$17,983**	**$18,002**	**$18,307**	**$18,837**	**$21,377**
($3,694)	**($3,601)**	**($2,953)**	**($2,683)**	**($102)**	**$1,793**	**$4,863**	**$4,023**
$25,661	$22,060	$19,107	$16,425	$16,322	$18,116	$22,979	$27,002

BALANCE SHEET		Mth 1	Mth 2	Mth 3	Mth 4
Assets	Starting Balances				
Current Assets					
Cash	$36,200	$40,419	$36,950	$32,904	$29,354
Inventory	$3,000	$1,750	$1,450	$1,474	$1,568
Other Current Assets	$8,000	$8,000	$8,000	$8,000	$8,000
Total Current Assets	$47,200	$50,169	$46,400	$42,378	$38,922
Long-term Assets					
Long-term Assets	$4,000	$4,000	$4,000	$4,000	$4,000
Accumulated Depreciation	$0	$166	$332	$498	$664
Total Long-term Assets	$4,000	$3,834	$3,668	$3,502	$3,336
Total Assets	**$51,200**	**$54,003**	**$50,068**	**$45,880**	**$42,258**
Current Liabilities					
Accounts Payable	$0	$8,155	$9,119	$9,468	$9,615
Current Borrowing	$0	$0	$0	$0	$0
Other Current Liabilities	$13,600	$13,300	$13,000	$12,700	$12,400
Subtotal Current Liabilities	$13,600	$21,455	$22,119	$22,168	$22,015
Long-term Liabilities	$15,400	$15,100	$14,800	$14,500	$14,200
Total Liabilities	**$29,000**	**$36,555**	**$36,919**	**$36,668**	**$36,215**
Paid-in Capital	$48,500	$48,500	$48,500	$48,500	$48,500
Retained Earnings	($26,300)	($26,300)	($26,300)	($26,300)	($26,300)
Earnings	$0	($4,752)	($9,051)	($12,988)	($16,157)
Total Capital	**$22,200**	**$17,448**	**$13,149**	**$9,212**	**$6,043**
Total Liabilities and Capital	**$51,200**	**$54,003**	**$50,068**	**$45,880**	**$42,258**
Net Worth	**$22,200**	**$17,448**	**$13,149**	**$9,212**	**$6,043**

Mth 5	Mth 6	Mth 7	Mth 8	Mth 9	Mth 10	Mth 11	Mth 12
$25,661	$22,060	$19,107	$16,425	$16,322	$18,116	$22,979	$27,002
$1,568	$1,568	$1,639	$1,683	$1,859	$2,211	$2,607	$2,794
$8,000	$8,000	$8,000	$8,000	$8,000	$8,000	$8,000	$8,000
$35,228	$31,628	$28,746	$26,108	$26,181	$28,327	$33,586	$37,796
$4,000	$4,000	$4,000	$4,000	$4,000	$4,000	$4,000	$4,000
$830	$996	$1,162	$1,328	$1,494	$1,660	$1,826	$1,992
$3,170	$3,004	$2,838	$2,672	$2,506	$2,340	$2,174	$2,008
$38,398	**$34,632**	**$31,584**	**$28,780**	**$28,687**	**$30,667**	**$35,760**	**$39,804**
$9,522	$9,520	$9,650	$9,659	$9,947	$10,424	$11,972	$11,731
$0	$0	$0	$0	$1,000	$1,000	$1,000	$0
$12,100	$11,800	$11,500	$11,200	$10,900	$10,600	$10,300	$10,000
$21,622	$21,320	$21,150	$20,859	$21,847	$22,024	$23,272	$21,731
$13,900	$13,600	$13,300	$13,000	$12,700	$12,400	$12,100	$11,800
$35,522	**$34,920**	**$34,450**	**$33,859**	**$34,547**	**$34,424**	**$35,372**	**$33,531**
$48,500	$48,500	$48,500	$48,500	$48,500	$48,500	$48,500	$48,500
($26,300)	($26,300)	($26,300)	($26,300)	($26,300)	($26,300)	($26,300)	($26,300)
($19,324)	($22,489)	($25,065)	($27,280)	($28,060)	($25,958)	($21,813)	($15,927)
$2,876	**($289)**	**($2,865)**	**($5,080)**	**($5,860)**	**($3,758)**	**$387**	**$6,273**
$38,398	**$34,632**	**$31,584**	**$28,780**	**$28,687**	**$30,667**	**$35,760**	**$39,804**
$2,876	**($289)**	**($2,865)**	**($5,080)**	**($5,860)**	**($3,758)**	**$387**	**$6,273**

CHAPTER 8

"The price of excellence is discipline. The cost of mediocrity is disappointment."

William Arthur Ward, Author

THIS CHAPTER COVERS:
DESCRIBING THE BUSINESS CONCEPT WORKSHEET
PRODUCT MARKETABILITY ANALYSIS SCORE SHEET
INDUSTRY ANALYSIS WORKSHEET
COMPETITOR ANALYSIS WORKSHEET
IDENTIFYING COMPETITIVE ADVANTAGES WORKSHEET

Describing the Business Concept Worksheet

This worksheet will serve as a guide to outline the basics of your business: the overall concept, industry in which the business will operate in, the clients it will serve, and the profits it will make.

In depth description from this worksheet will subsequently lead to further analysis in the main body of the business plan and executive summary.

Instructions:

Describe the primary features of the business concept

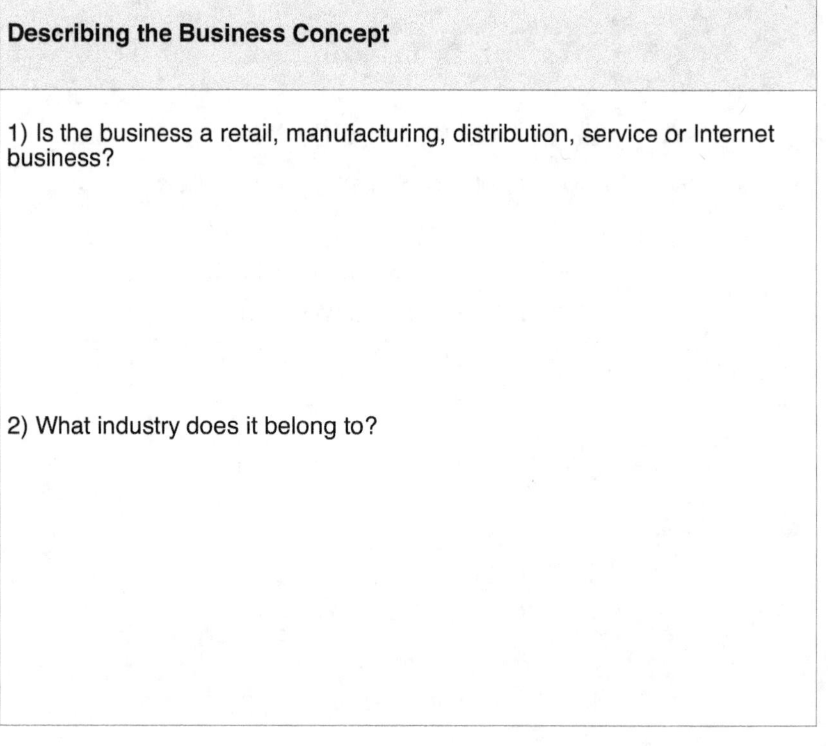

3) What are the products or services?

4) Who are the potential customers?

5) How will they be reached?

6) Who are your competitors?

A. Product Marketability Analysis Score Sheet

Research the marketability of the product/ service.

Assumption that a great idea will or can generate profit is simply delusional if there is no underlying evidence to rationalize such assumption.

There must be succinct information that there are willing clients who are prepared to pay for the product/ service.

Instructions:

- Plan four different product/service concepts - each similar, but with variations.

- Score each of them high, medium or low to find out whether the product/service is marketable.

	Product/ Service Concept 1	Product/ Service Concept 2	Product/ Service Concept 3	Product/ Service Concept 4
Probability of use by target market				
Compatibility with image desired				
Competitive-ness of price				
Number and strength of marketable features				
Probability that product will enhance sales of current line				
Projected stability of demand				

	Product/ Service Concept 1	Product/ Service Concept 2	Product/ Service Concept 3	Product/ Service Concept 4
Ability to overcome seasonal or cyclical resistance				
Uniqueness of product				
Ability of business to obtain needed equipment				
Likely acceptance potential				
Ability of business to afford the development and production of product				
Column Totals				

B. Industry Analysis Worksheet

Use this checklist to help you define your position in your industry and identify possible niche markets for your product.

Industry Analysis Checklist

This checklist can be used to help you define your position in your industry and identify possible niche markets for your product.

This information will be critical for the Industry Analysis section of your business plan.

Instructions:

- Ensure you have the answers and back-up research for the following questions:

	Are there any new competitors in the arena? Does everyone think this is a hot idea?
	Has any gone out of business recently? Why?
	If there have been no new entries in the market, is it because there are fatal flaws with the concept, or because you are the first with a new idea? Have you figured out how to overcome problems others didn't solve?
	Are there a small number of competitors for a large market, or a large number for a small market?
	If all the other competitors are large companies, can you fit in a small but profitable niche, or do you have the capital to compete head-to-head? Are you at risk of being attacked by large, established corporations?
	If there had been no recent innovation in your market, is it because the profit margins aren't there to make it profitable, or because the corporations are getting lazy and staid and giving you a legitimate opportunity?
	Is there room for improvement in the quality f service given to the market (for example, the Postal Service), which will give a new/small company an edge?
	What is the history of your market? New markets, like microwaveable foods when microwaves were first invented, grow and change quickly. Old markets, like radio manufacturing, may be more difficult to enter. In an old market you must have a new idea, a real edge. In a new market, you need to be fast.

C. Competitor Analysis Worksheet

This worksheet will help you define your competitors, pin-point their present position and outline their strengths and weaknesses.

Competitor Analysis Worksheet

Competitors are companies that make products or perform services similar to yours (e.g. you deliver complete dinners, and so do they), make products or perform services that can be substituted for yours (e.g. delivery of pizza or Chinese food), and make products or perform services that are analogous to yours (e.g. ready-made deli take-always from supermarkets).

Instructions:

- Fill in the following table about your competitors.

- You may need to create additional tables to have enough room for all your major competitors.

	Competitor A	Competitor B	Competitor C
Where is your competitor located?			
What are your competitor's annual sales?			
Who are the major managers and members of the board?			
Is the company owned or in partnership with any other corporations?			
What are the competitor's strengths?			

What are their weaknesses?			
What is the company's product line?			
How do the products compare to yours, in terms of functionality, appearance and any other criteria?			
What is their price structure?			
What are the company's marketing activities?			
What are the company's supply sources for products?			
What are the strengths and weaknesses of their sales literature?			
Is the company expanding or cutting back?			

D. Identifying Competitive Advantages Worksheet

What are your competitive advantages? Use this work sheet to help you figure them out.

Identifying Competitive Advantages Worksheet

Identifying the Competitive Advantages
1) Are you offering new product/s or service/s?
2) Are you offering improved product/s or service/s?
3) Do you reach new or underserved markets?

4) Can you usher in new delivery systems?

What makes you different from competitors offering similar products or services? You'll need to address this in your business plan.

Instructions:

- List the advantages that you have in any of the following areas:

]

CONCLUSION

"Destiny is not a matter of chance, it is a matter of choice; it is not a thing to be waited for, it is a thing to be achieved."

Winston Churchill, former British Prime Minister

Now that you have the basic building blocks of a business plan, it is up to you to write one for your company. As you know, a business plan will help you to focus on what matters most – running a profitable enterprise. You will use your plan to make the best decisions in operations, management, marketing, and solicitation of investment funds. Use your business plan to put your best foot forward.

Know also that your business plan is one of the things you need to run a successful business. In addition, you need to keep acquiring the education, skills, and experience that will promote the wellbeing of your business. In light of this, I recommend to you, my books: *The Entrepreneurial Revolution: A Solution for Poverty Eradication, Identify and Fund your Business*, and *Why and How You Start your Business*. Also visit me on the web for more useful tips to run a successful business. Go for gold!

African Entrepreneurs
www.theafricanentrepreneurs.com
REGISTER NOW FOR
▸ Free tax information
▸ Tips on entrepreneurship
▸ Free newsletter
▸ Investments in Africa
▸ Business promotion
Meet other entrepreneurs from Africa.
Business networking, discussion forums,
contacts, advertisements and investments.
www.theafricanentrepreneurs.com

Nigerian Entrepreneurs

Register now @

www.nigerian-entrepreneur.com

FOR FREE

- Business Information
- E-Book & Newsletter
- Business Tips
- Tax Information

- Business Networking
- Social Enterprise
- Business Directory
- News & Information

<u>**RESOURCES**</u>

Thank you for your Investment in 'How to Prepare a Business Plan: *A Step by Step Guide'*.

The following books are out now
-Why and How to Start your Own Business: *A Simple Guide for Business Start-ups*
-How to Identify and Fund your Business: *200 Business Ideas and 28 Ways to Raise Capital for Your Business*
-Success in your Business: *How to Become a successful Entrepreneur*
-Entrepreneurial Revolution: *Solution for Poverty Eradication*

For Entrepreneurial Workshops and Seminars contact: www.peterosalor.com

To Order Online HYPERLINK
"http://www.peterosalor.com/"http://www.peterosalor.com

<u>**Recommended Resources**</u>

Tax Advice and Consultancy, UK
Peter Osalor and Co.
 HYPERLINK "http://www.posagconsulting.com/"http://www.posagconsulting.com

<u>**Marketing Your Company**</u>

Web hosting
Hostgator HYPERLINK "http://secure.hostgator.com/~affiliat/cgi-bin/affiliates/clickthru.cgi?id=osalorp" \n _blankhttp://secure.hostgator.com/~affiliat/cgi-bin/affiliates/clickthru.cgi?id=osalorp

Domain Registration & Hosting
1and 1 HYPERLINK "http://1and1.co.uk/?affiliate_id=237255" \n _blankhttp://1and1.co.uk/?affiliate_id=237255

E-Mail Marketing Software
Aweber HYPERLINK "http://www.aweber.com/?357303" \n _blankhttp://www.aweber.com/?357303

Get Response HYPERLINK
"http://www.getresponse.com/index/posalor"http://www.getresponse.com/index/posalor

Web Design and Marketing Company

London Top Web Design – London, UK
HYPERLINK
"http://www.webdesign.londontop.co.uk/"http://www.webdesign.londontop.co.uk
Internet Marketing and Coaching
New Dawn Concepts, London, UK
HYPERLINK http://www.adedalmeida.com/

Now that you know how to identify and fund your business why not purchase '*Success in your Business*' - volume four within the Entrepreneurial Development Series.

It's available online and in bookstores near you.

Purchase all the books within the *Entrepreneurial Development Series*.
They are available online and in bookstores near you.

Peter Osalor

ECONOMIC
TRANSFORMATION

*From a Poor Person to a Wealthy Person,
From a Poor Nation to a Wealthy Nation*

Entrepreneur, Entrepreneurship, Entrepreneulism,
MSME, Entrepreneurial Revolution

COMING SOON!

YOUTH
EMPOWERMENT
AND
ENTREPRENEURIAL
REVOLUTION
A Solution for Youth Restiveness,
Job Creation and a Prosperous Society
Peter Osalor

COMING SOON!

Women
Empowerment
& Entrepreneurial
Revolution
The solution for a prosperous society, poverty
eradication and wealth creation
Peter Osalor

COMING SOON!